I0409416

SARCASTIC COLORING BOOK FOR SENIORS

ADDING A SPLASH OF HUMOUR TO YOUR GOLDEN AGE

Russell Sylvester Byrne

GET MORE BOOKS FROM THE AUTHOR

Scan this with your Camera

THIS BOOK

BELONGS

TO

....

....

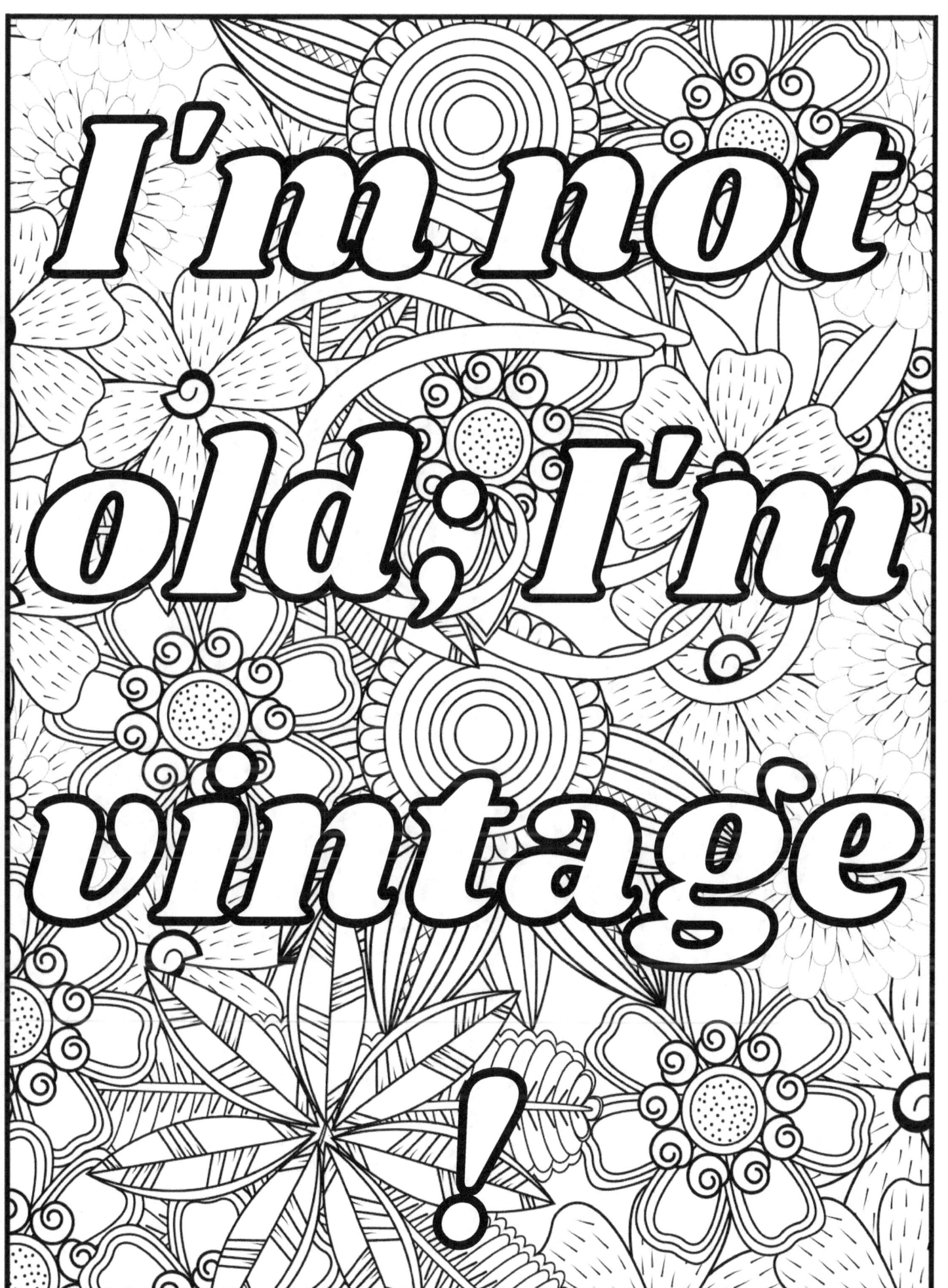

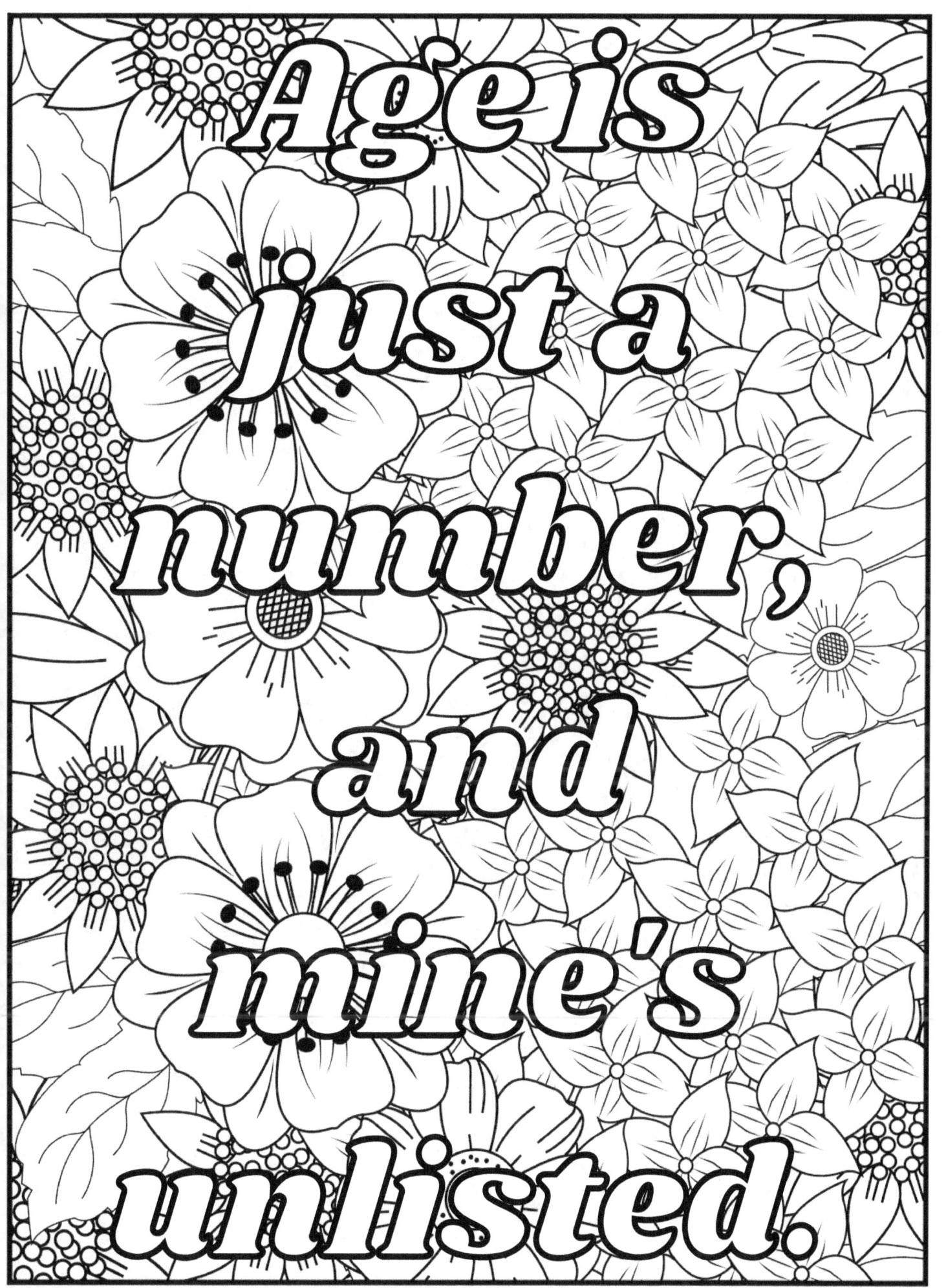

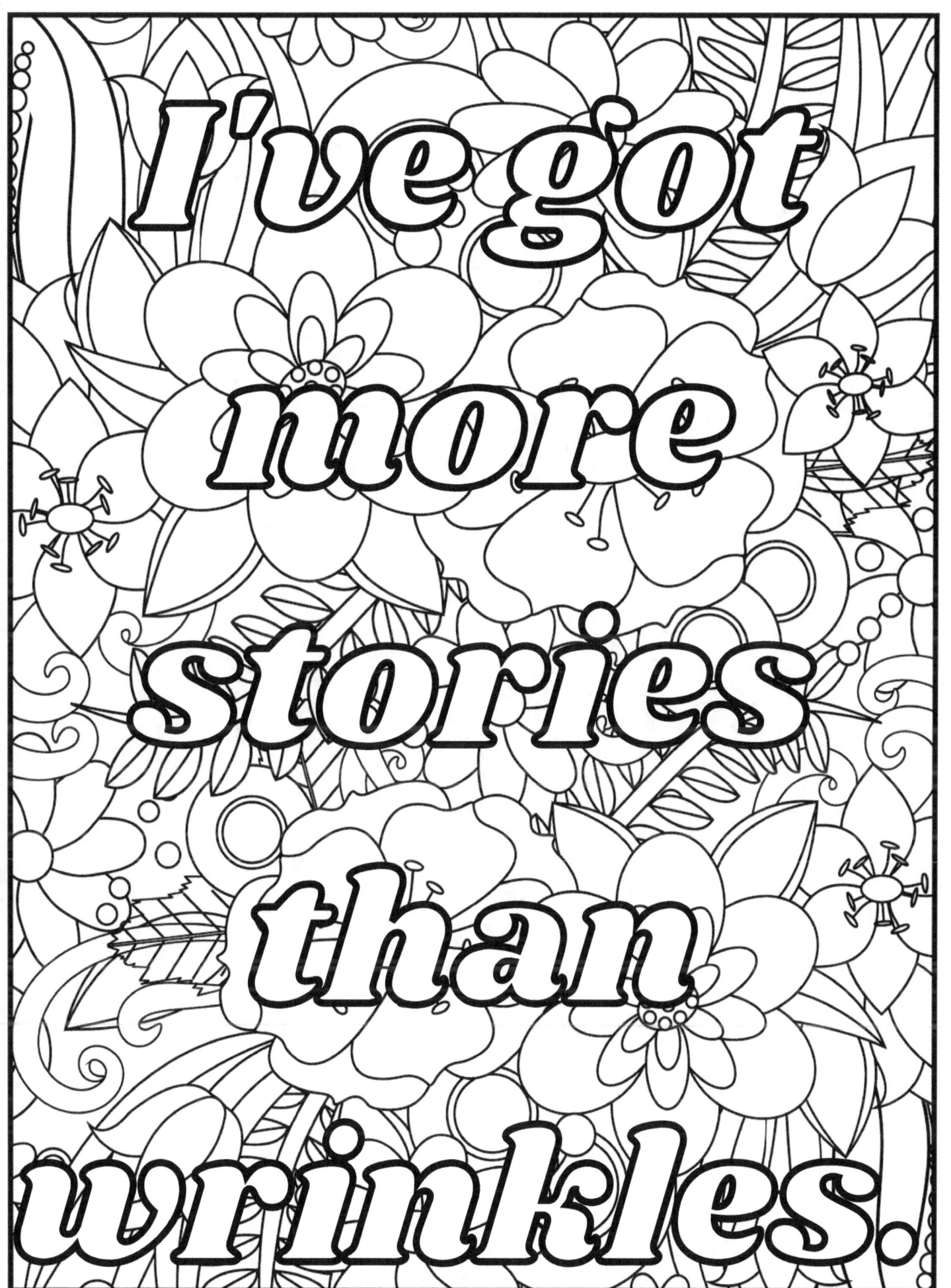

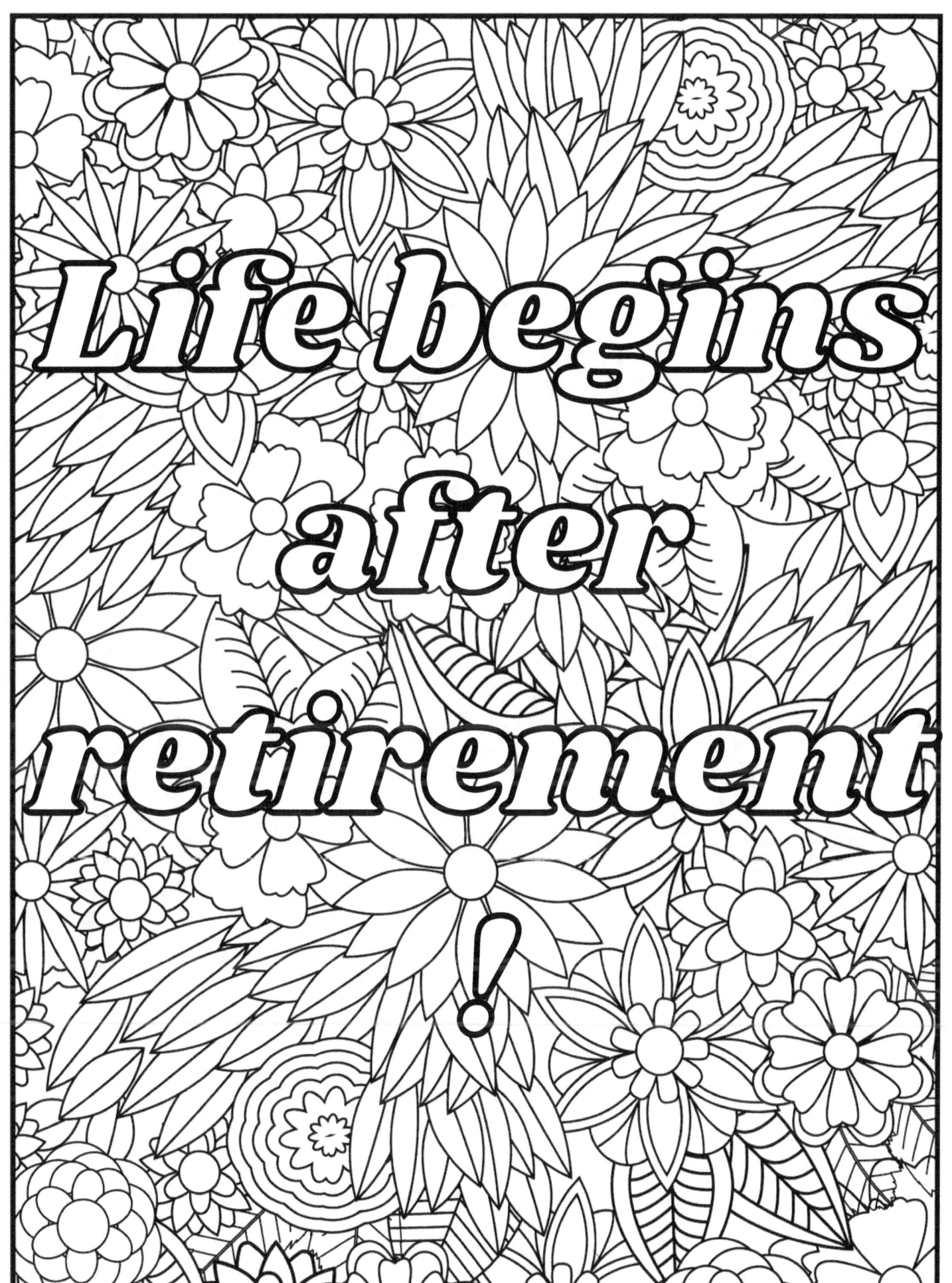

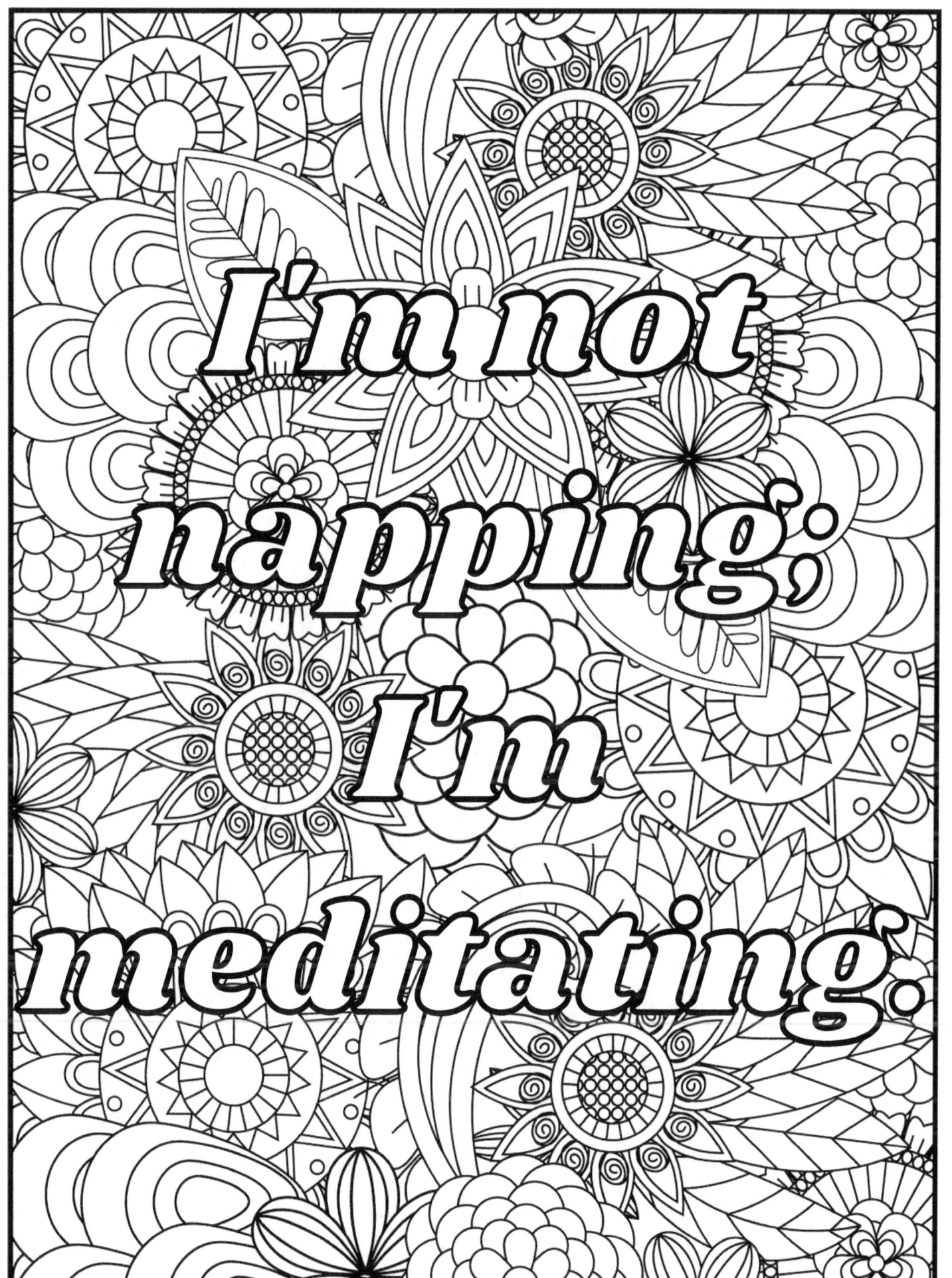

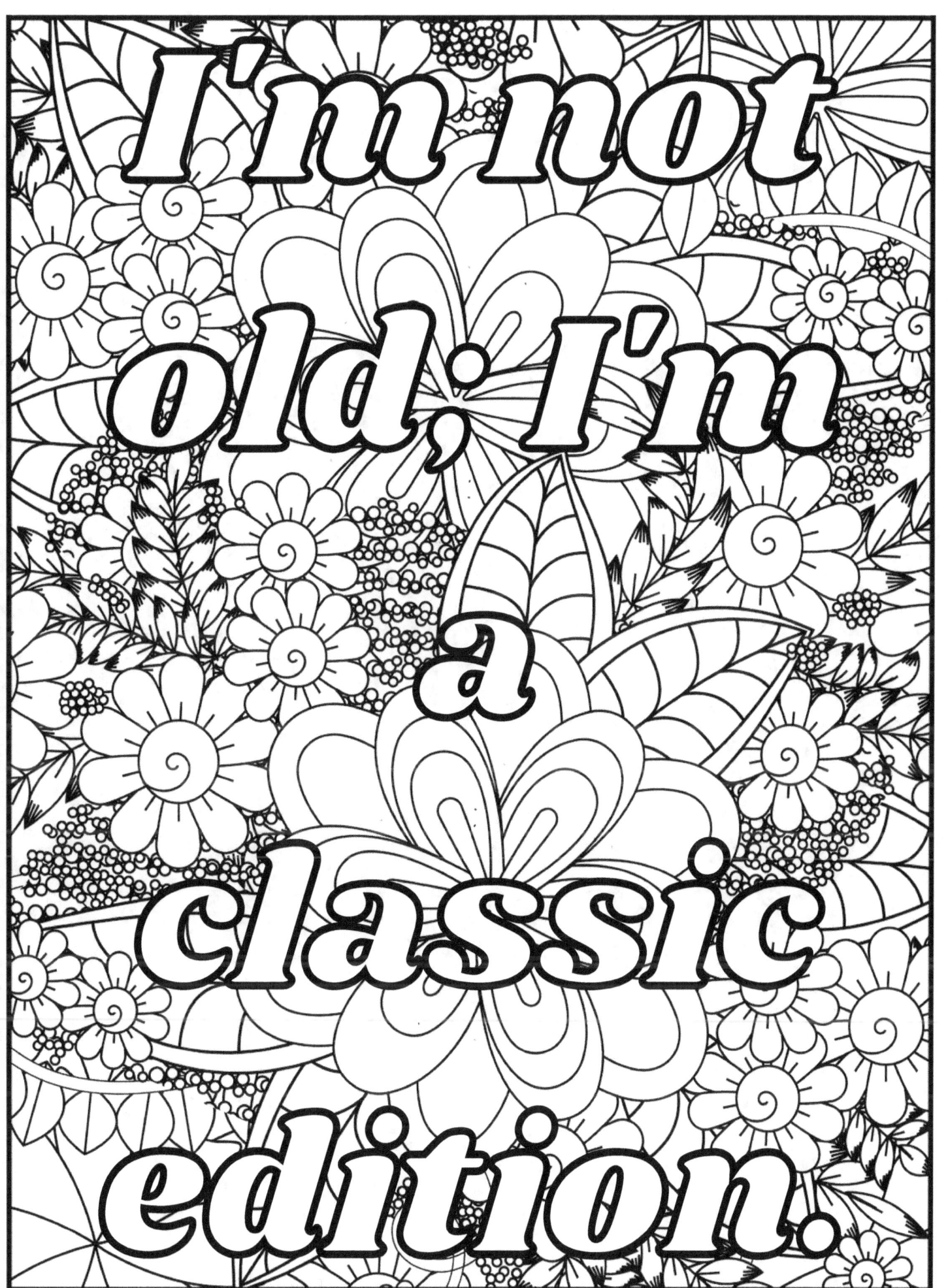

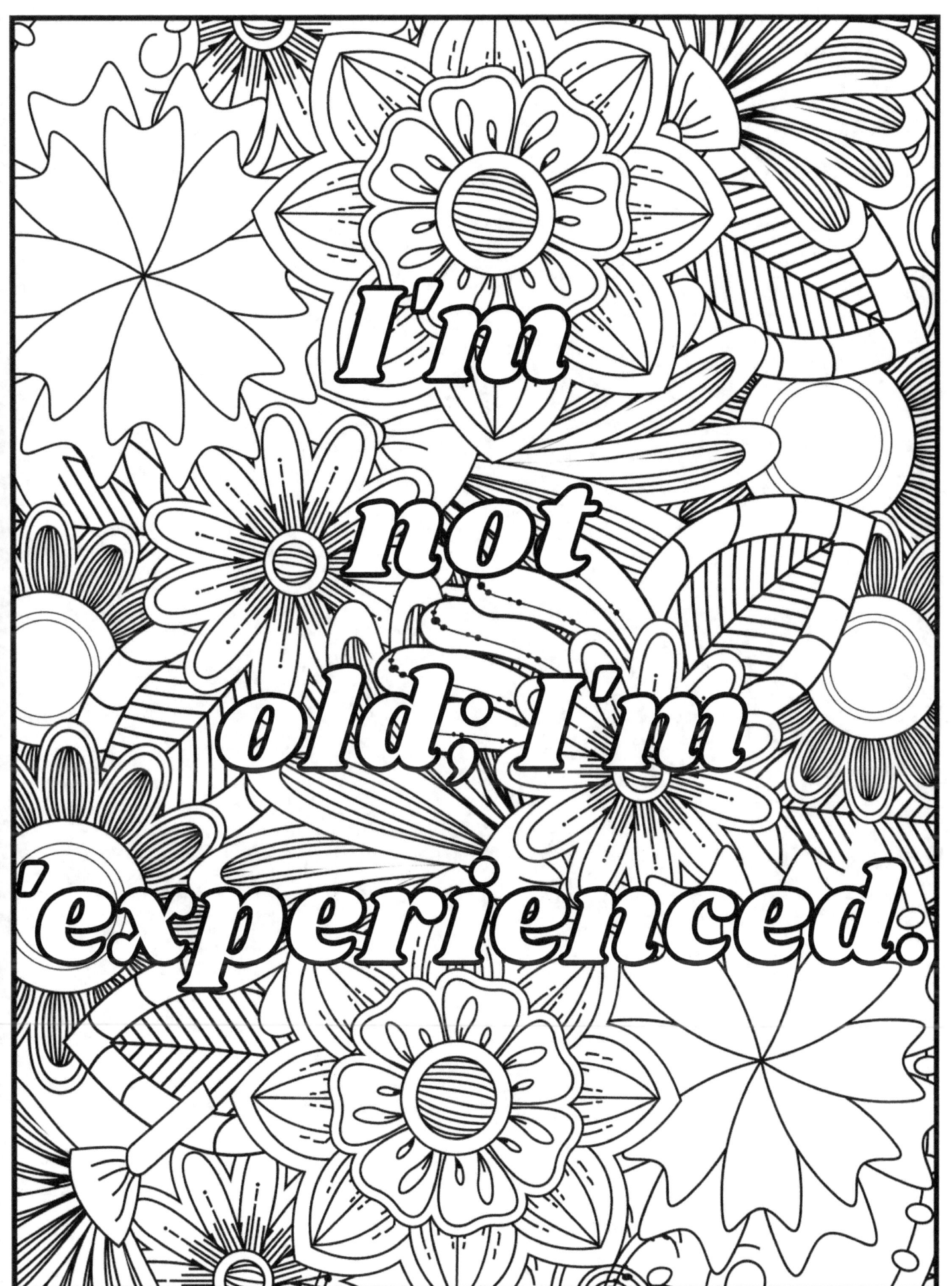

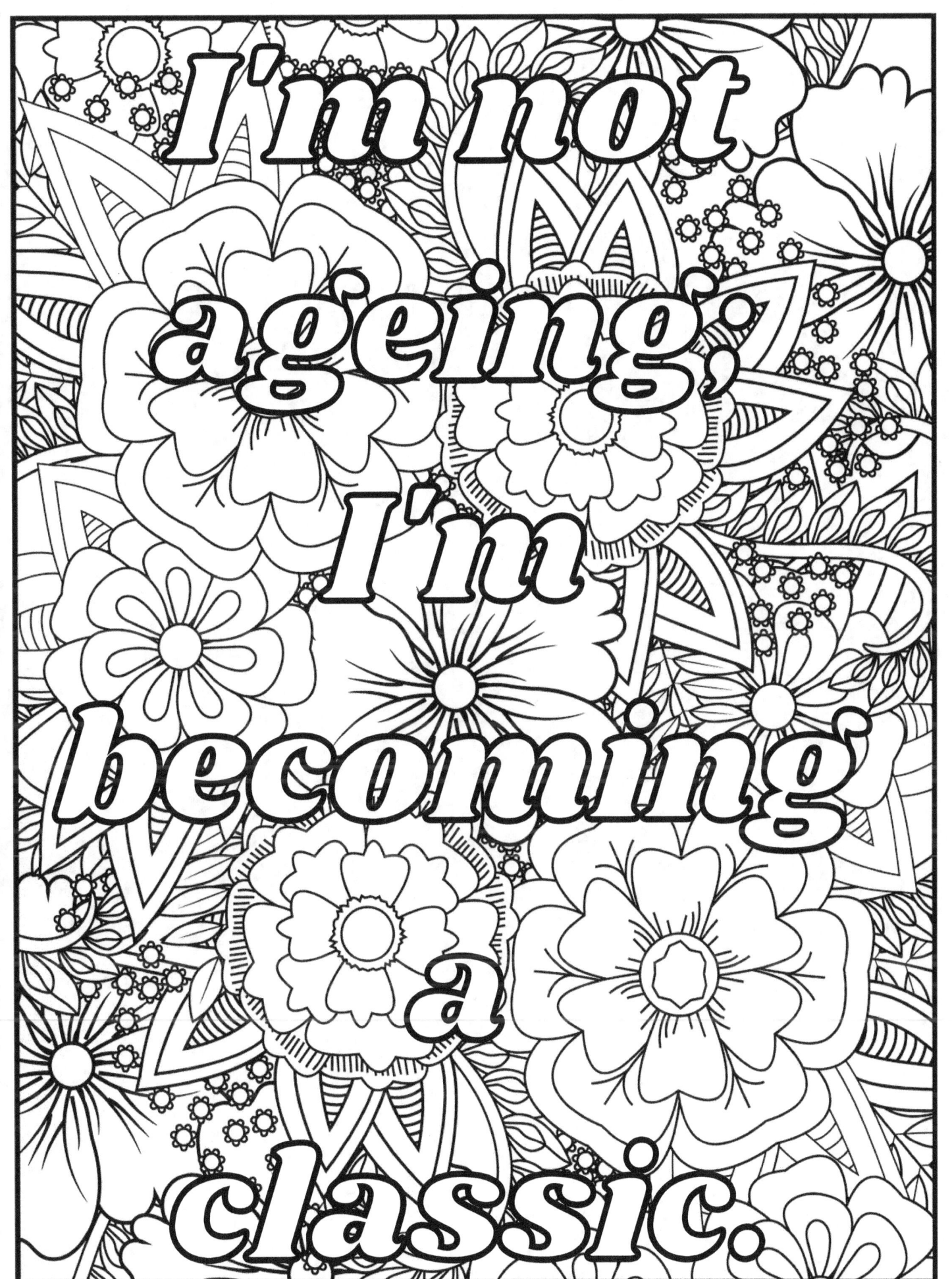

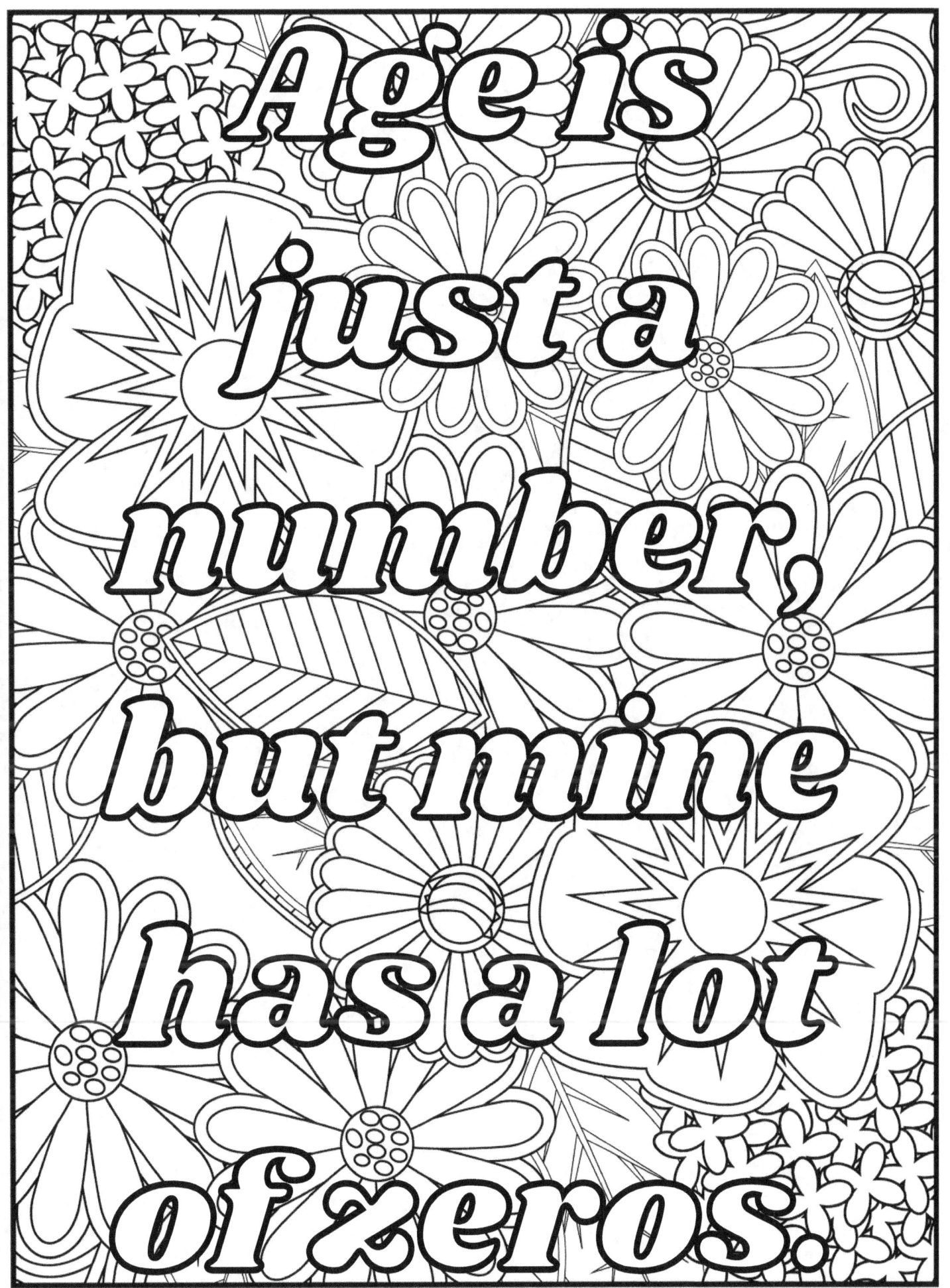

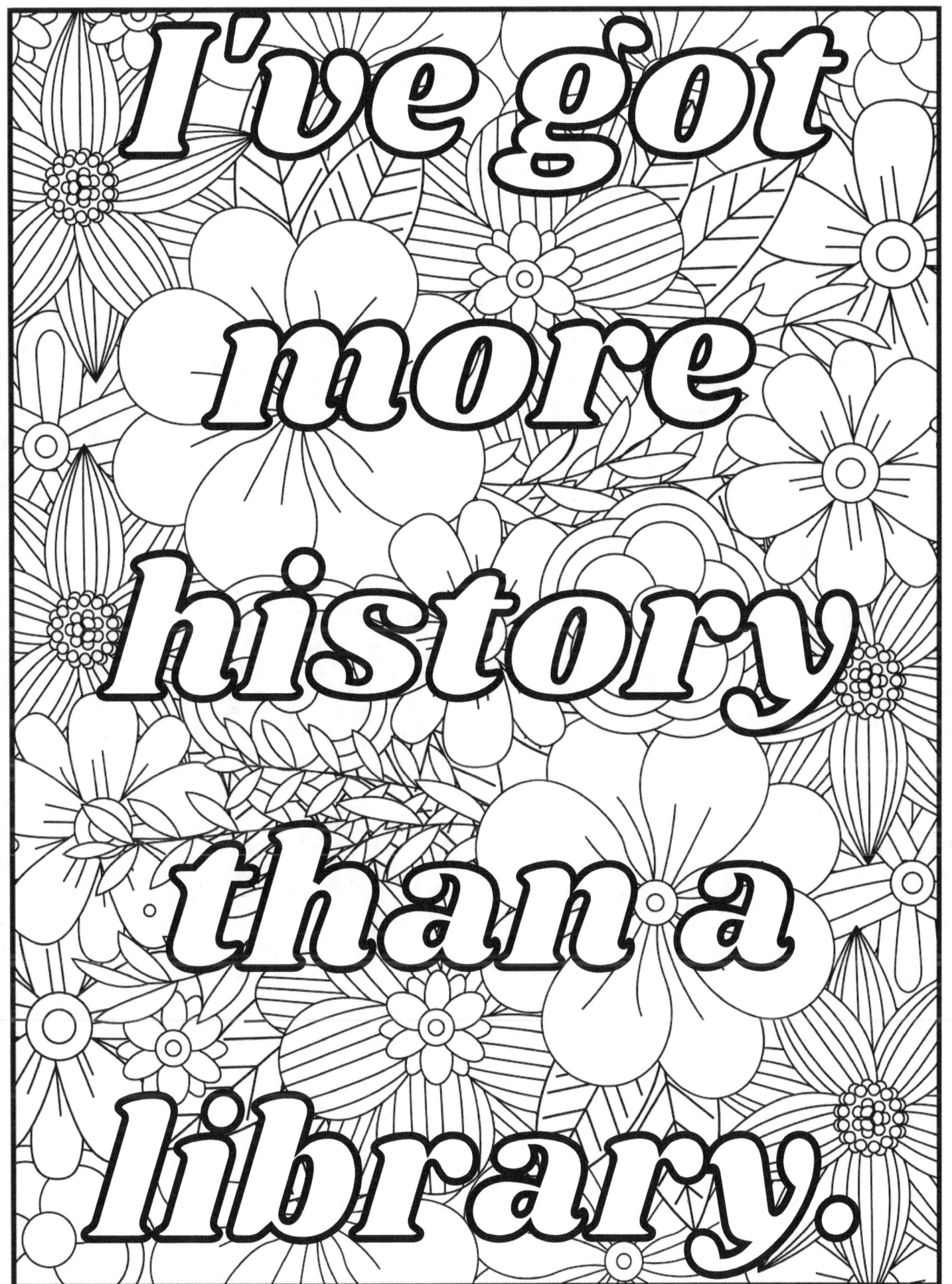

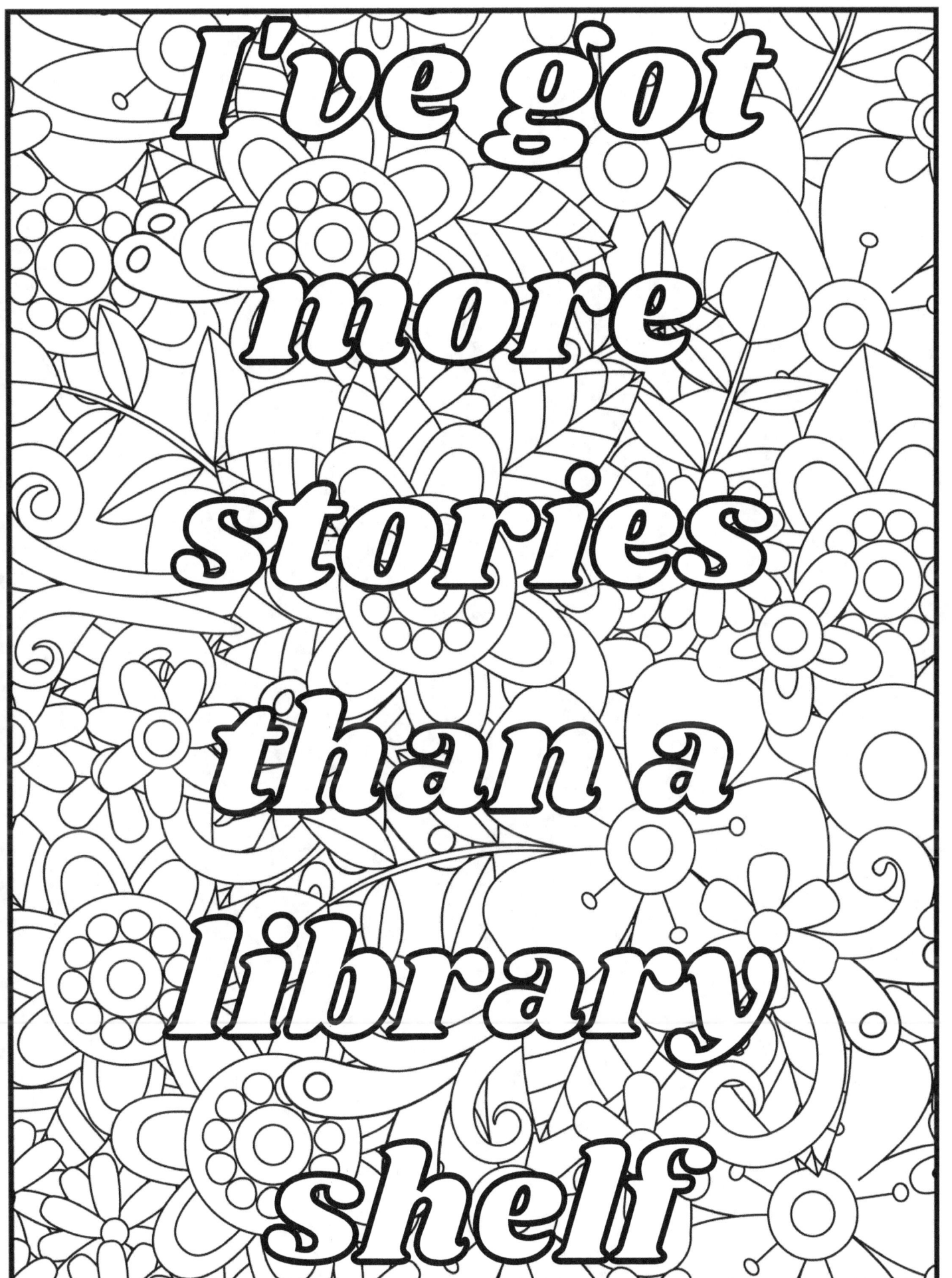

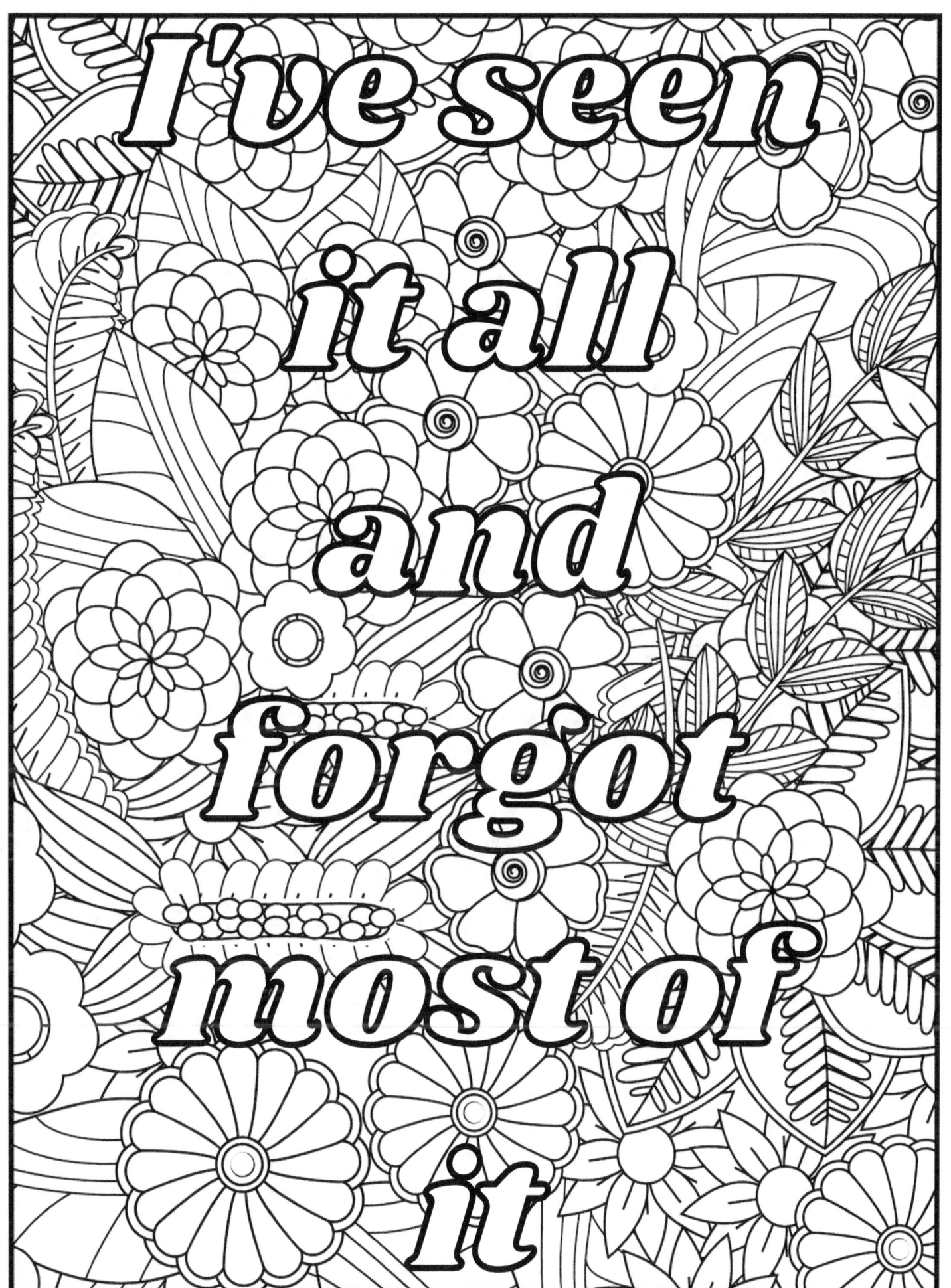

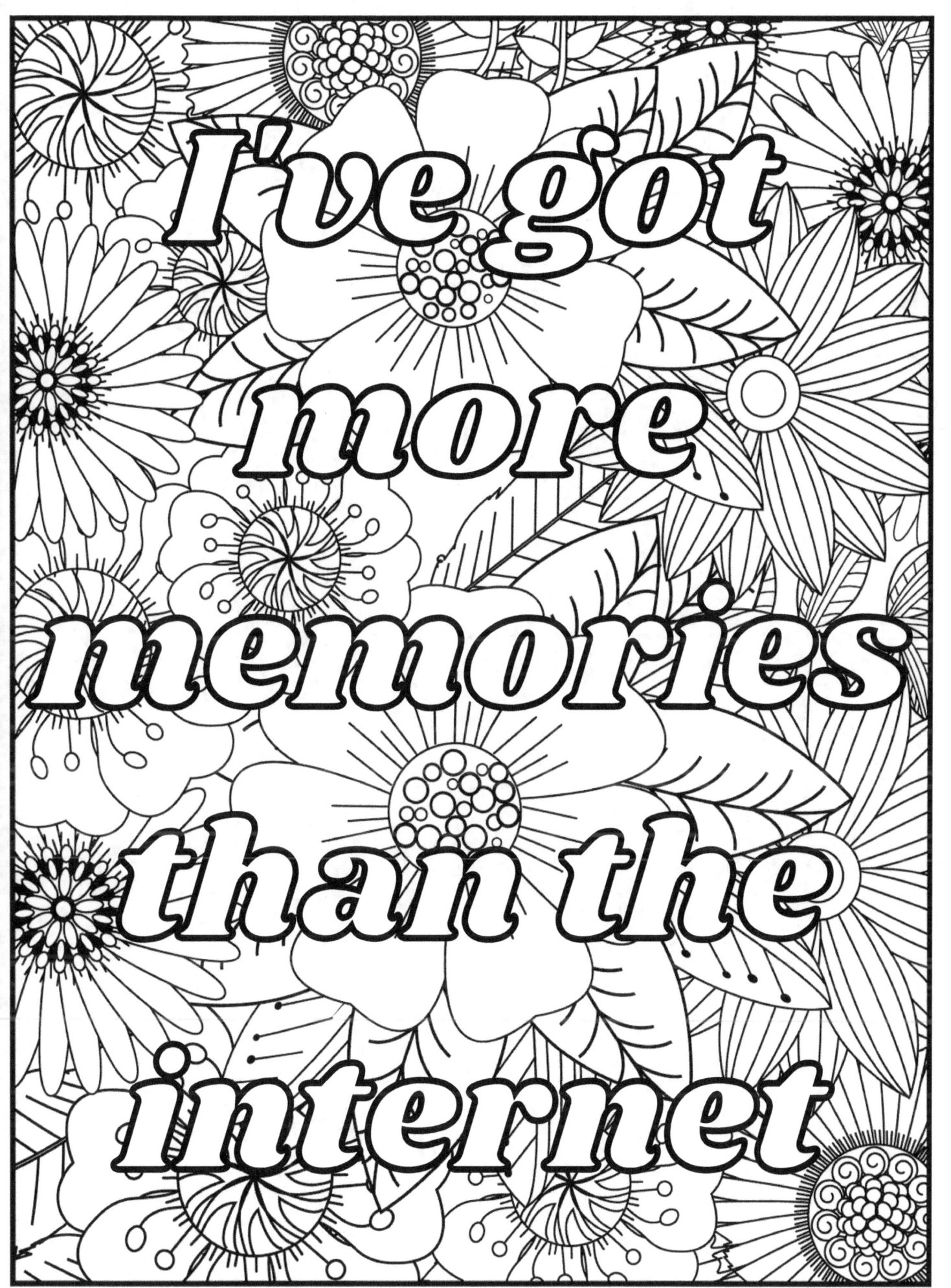

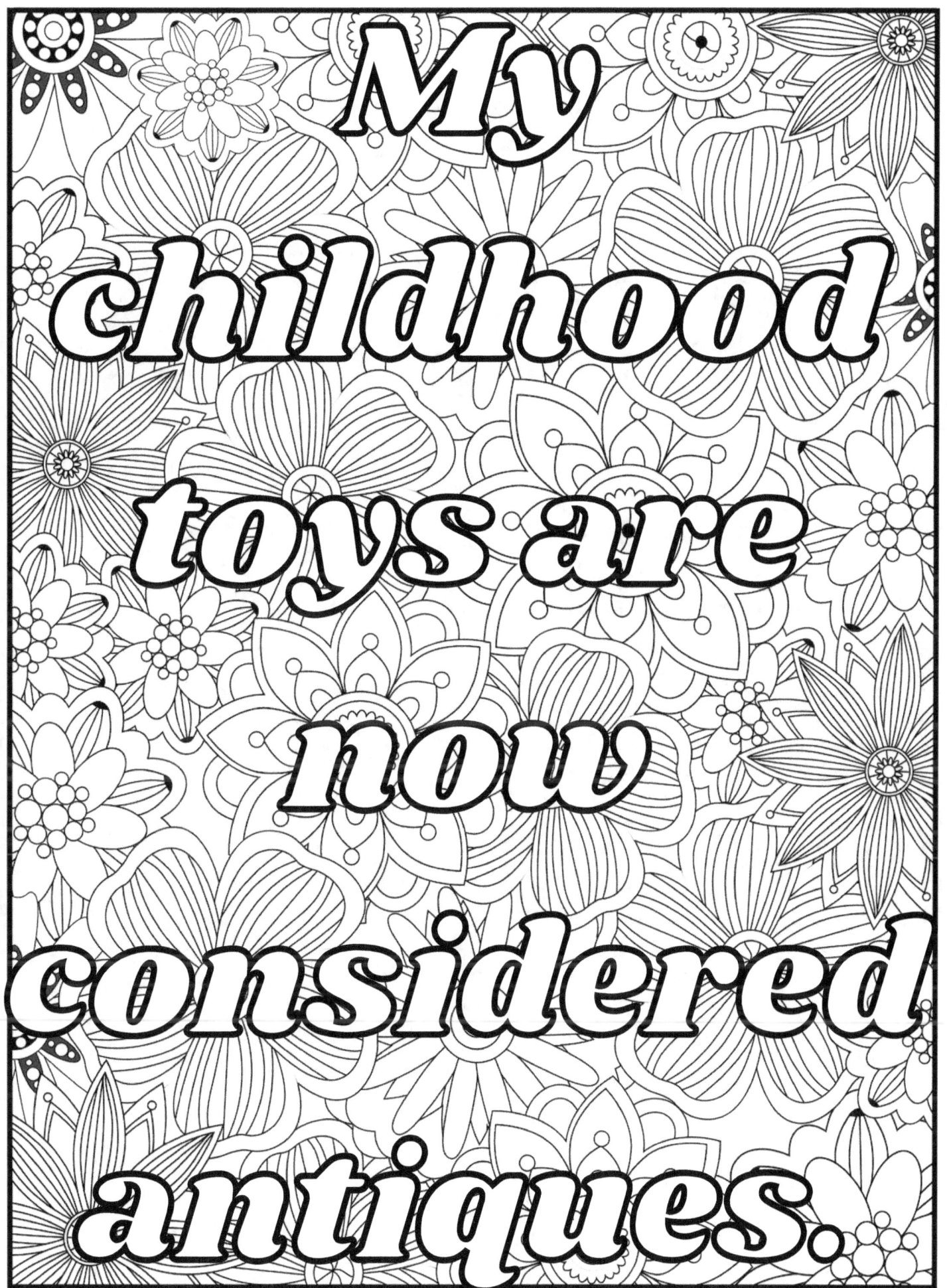

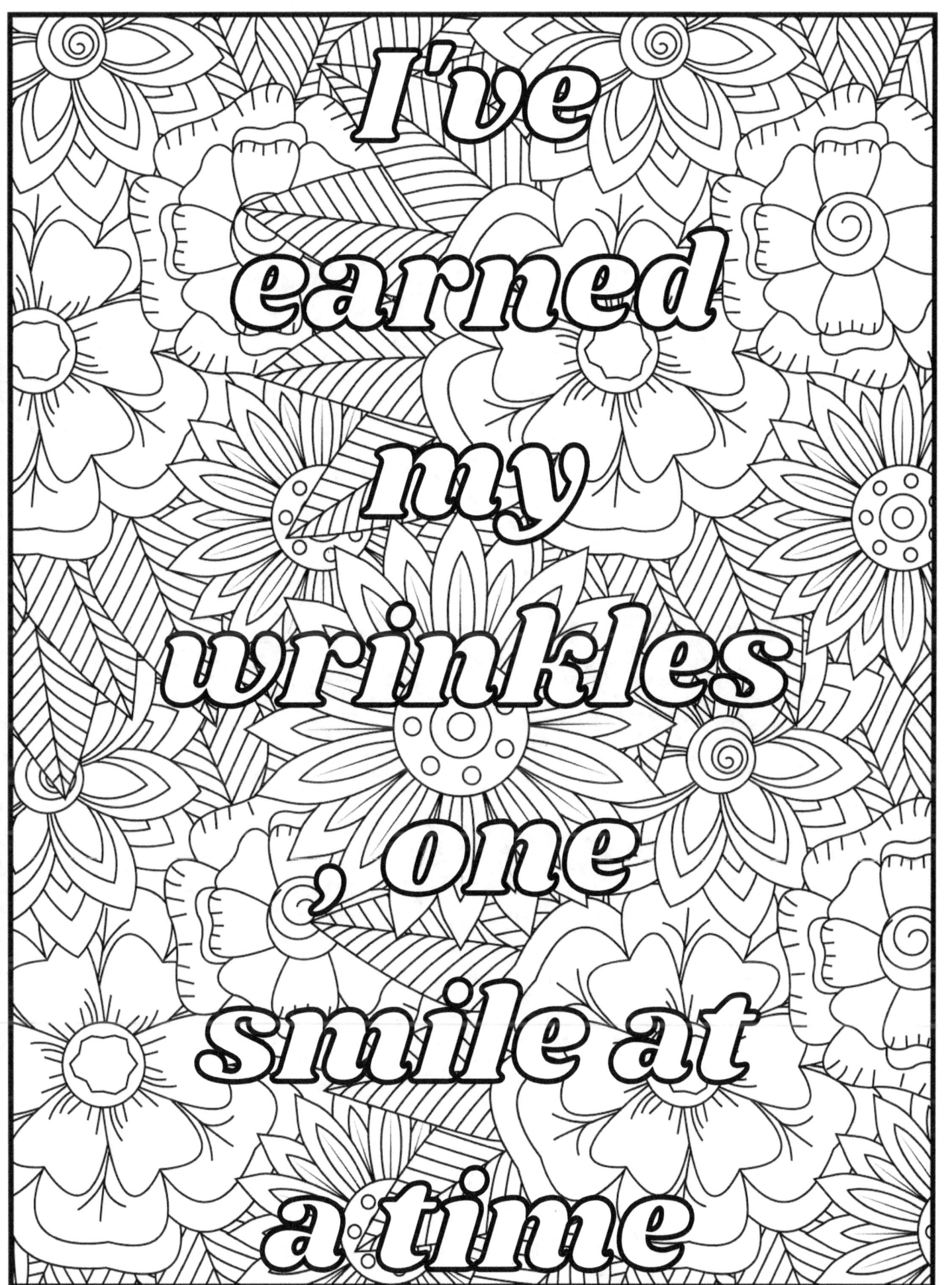

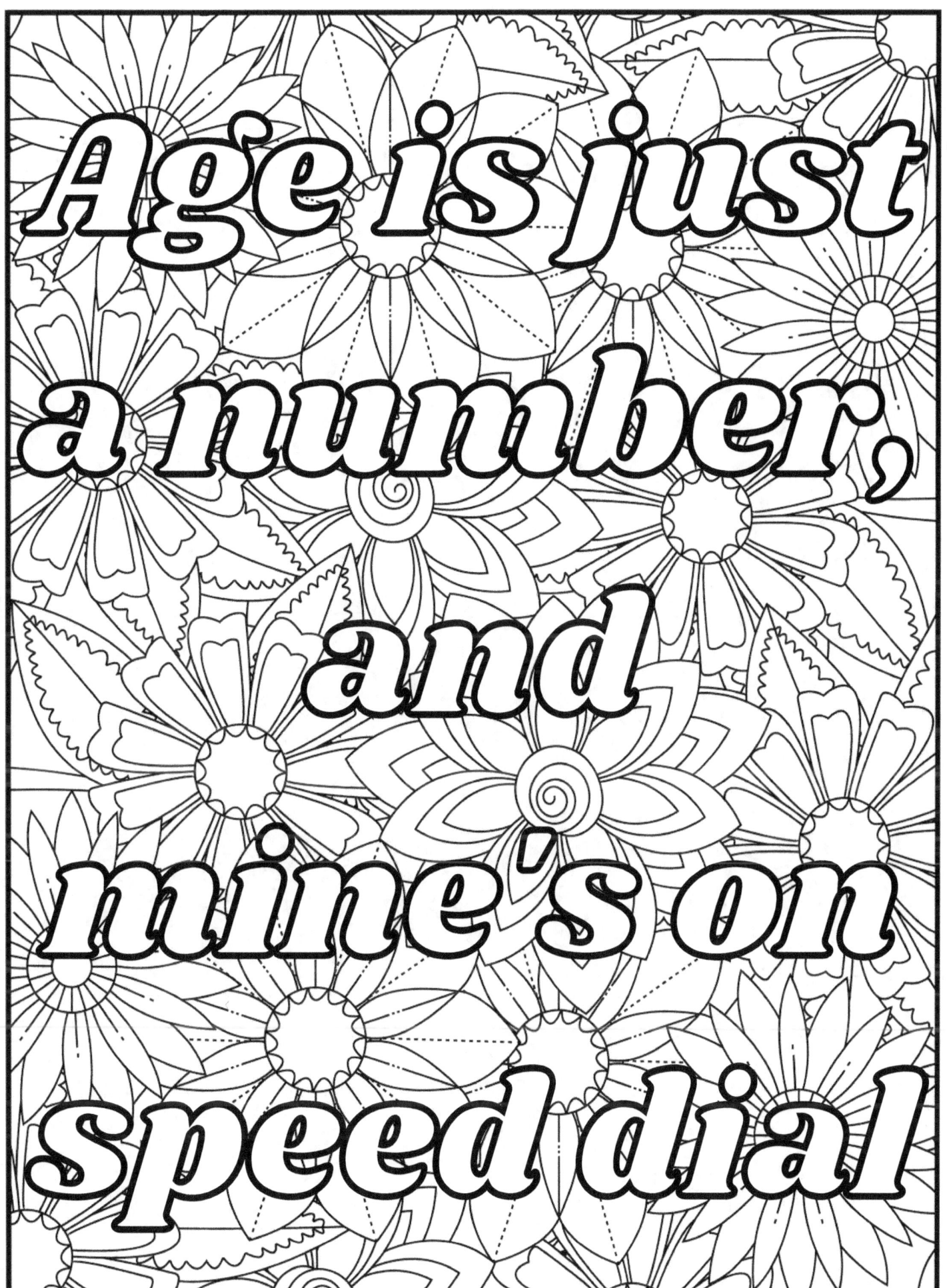

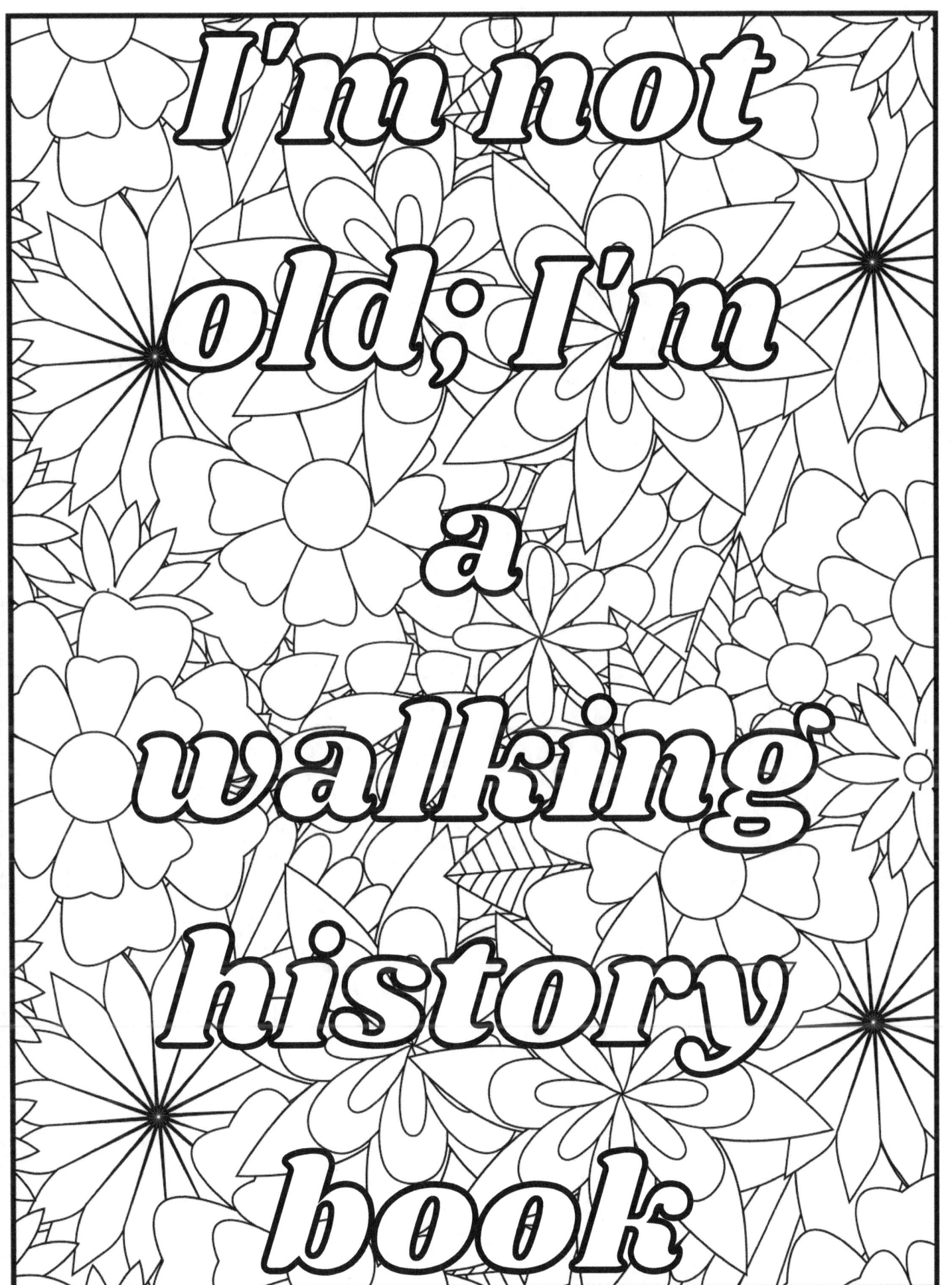

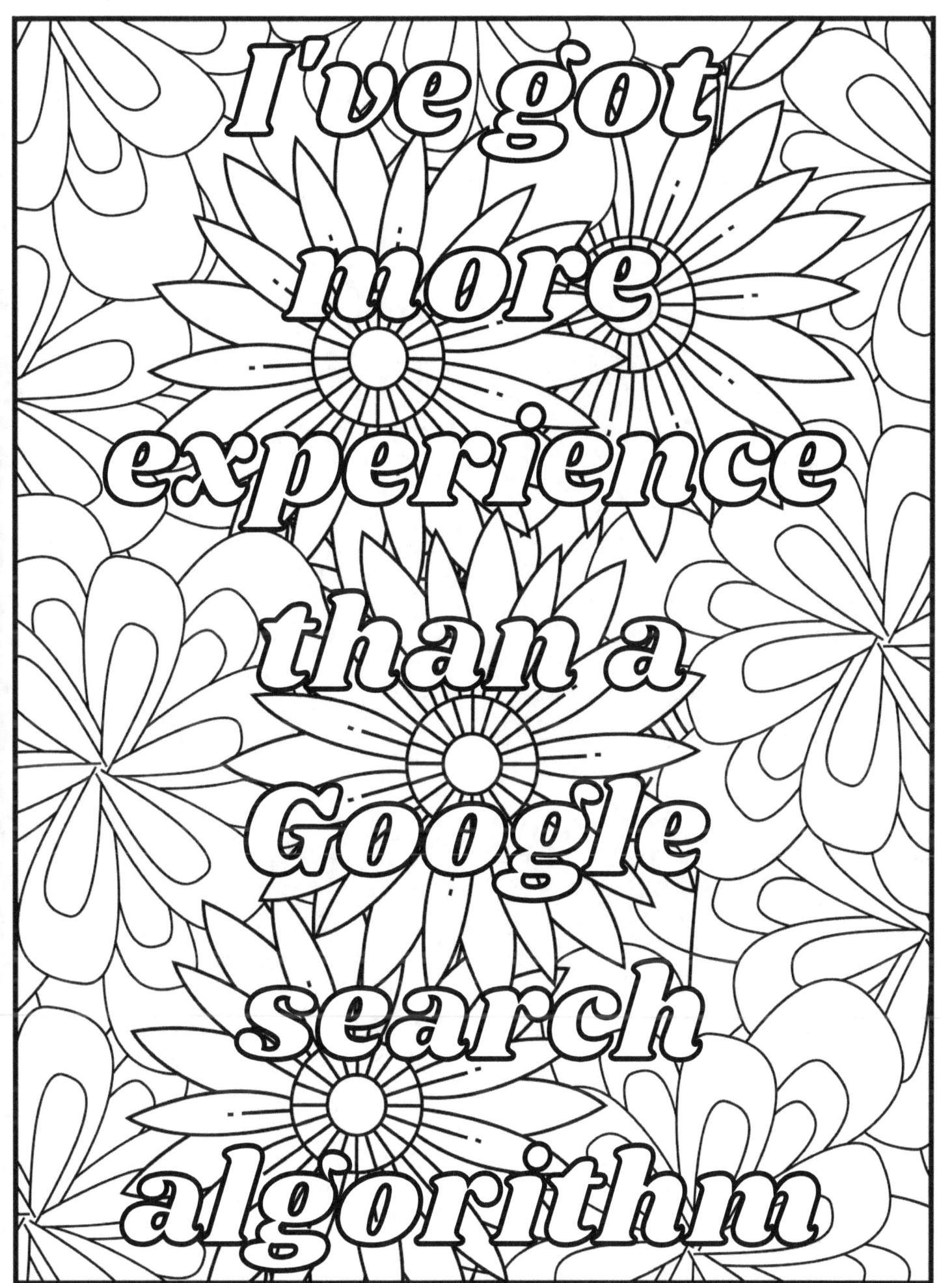

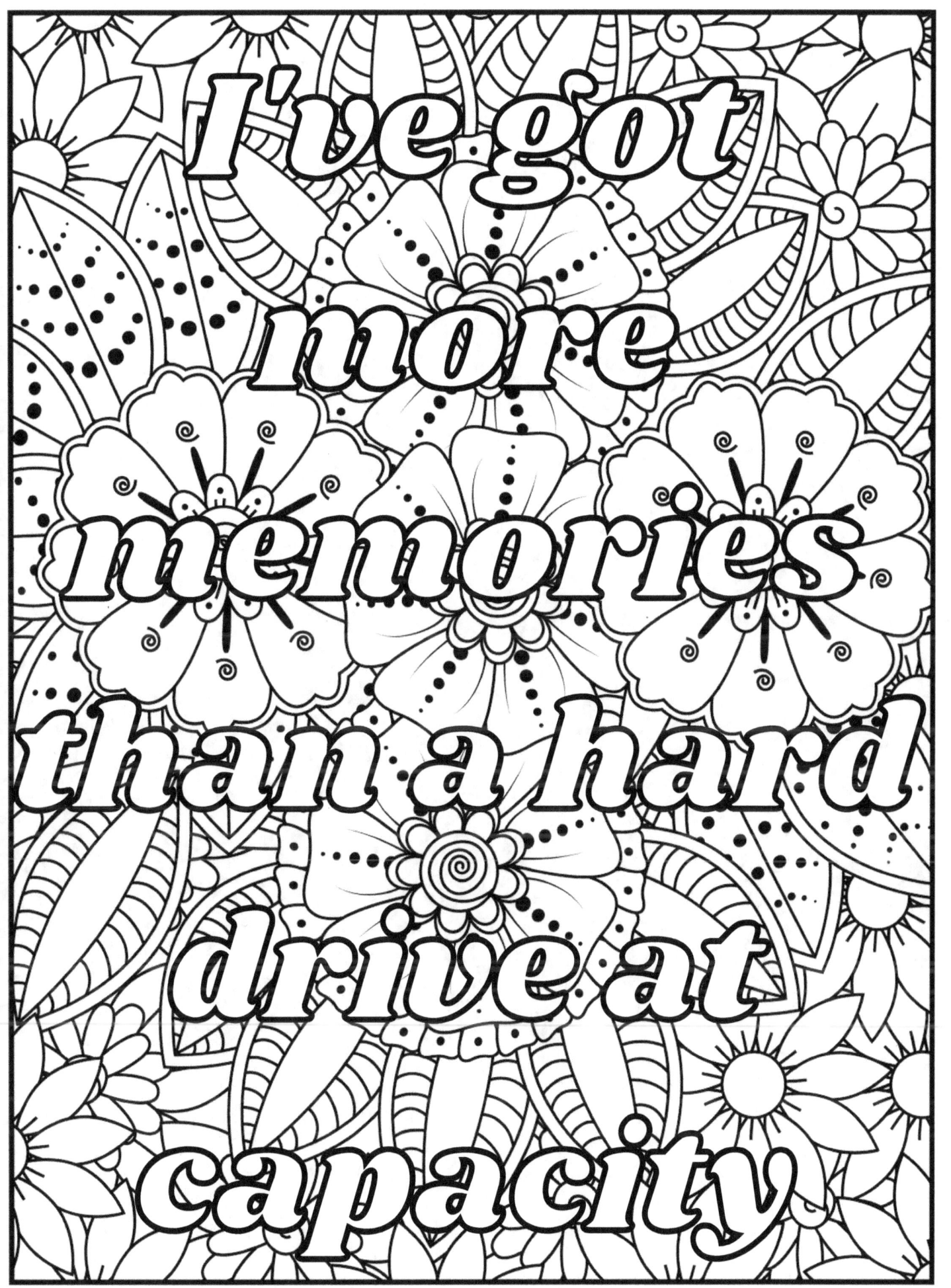

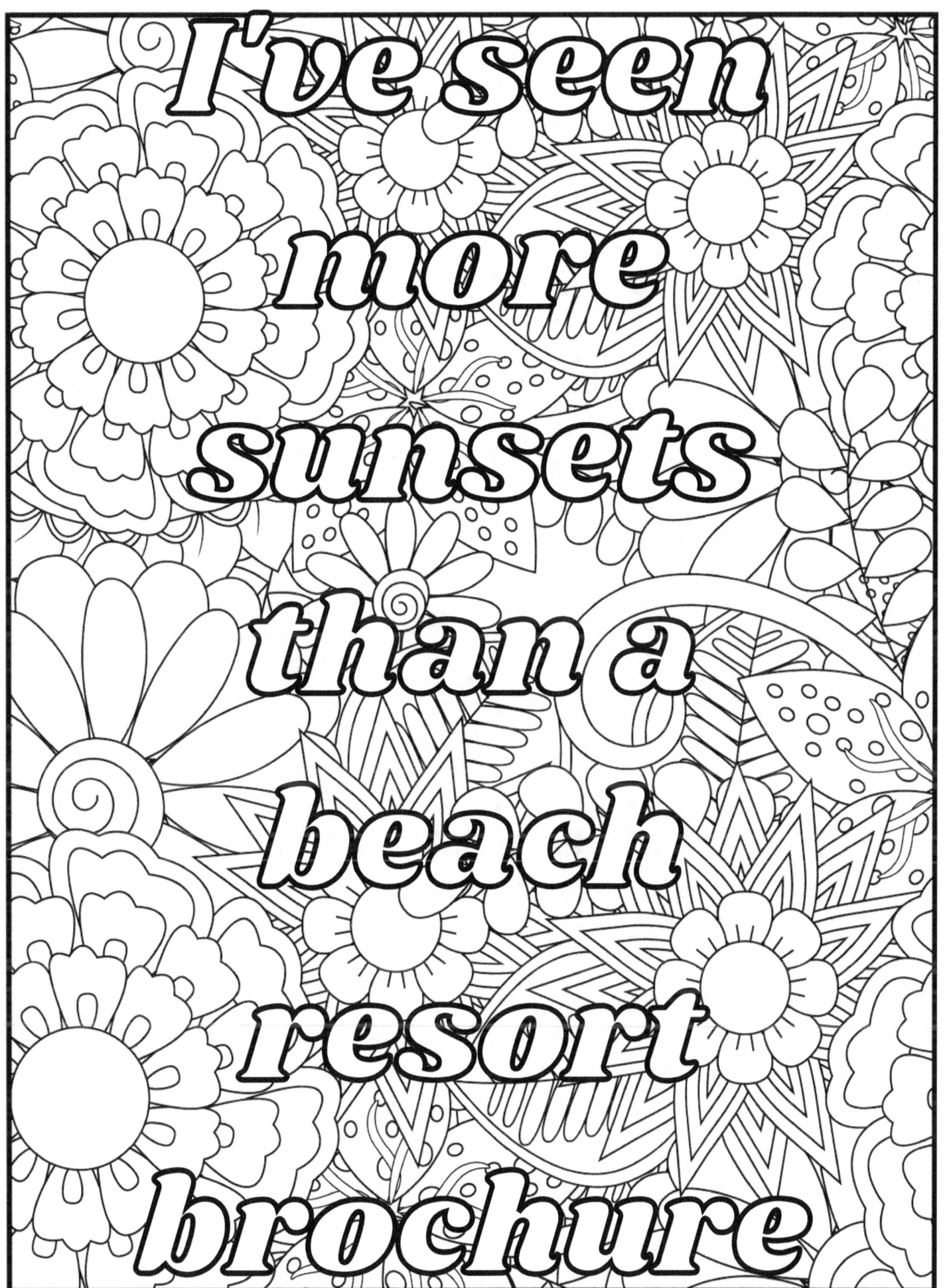

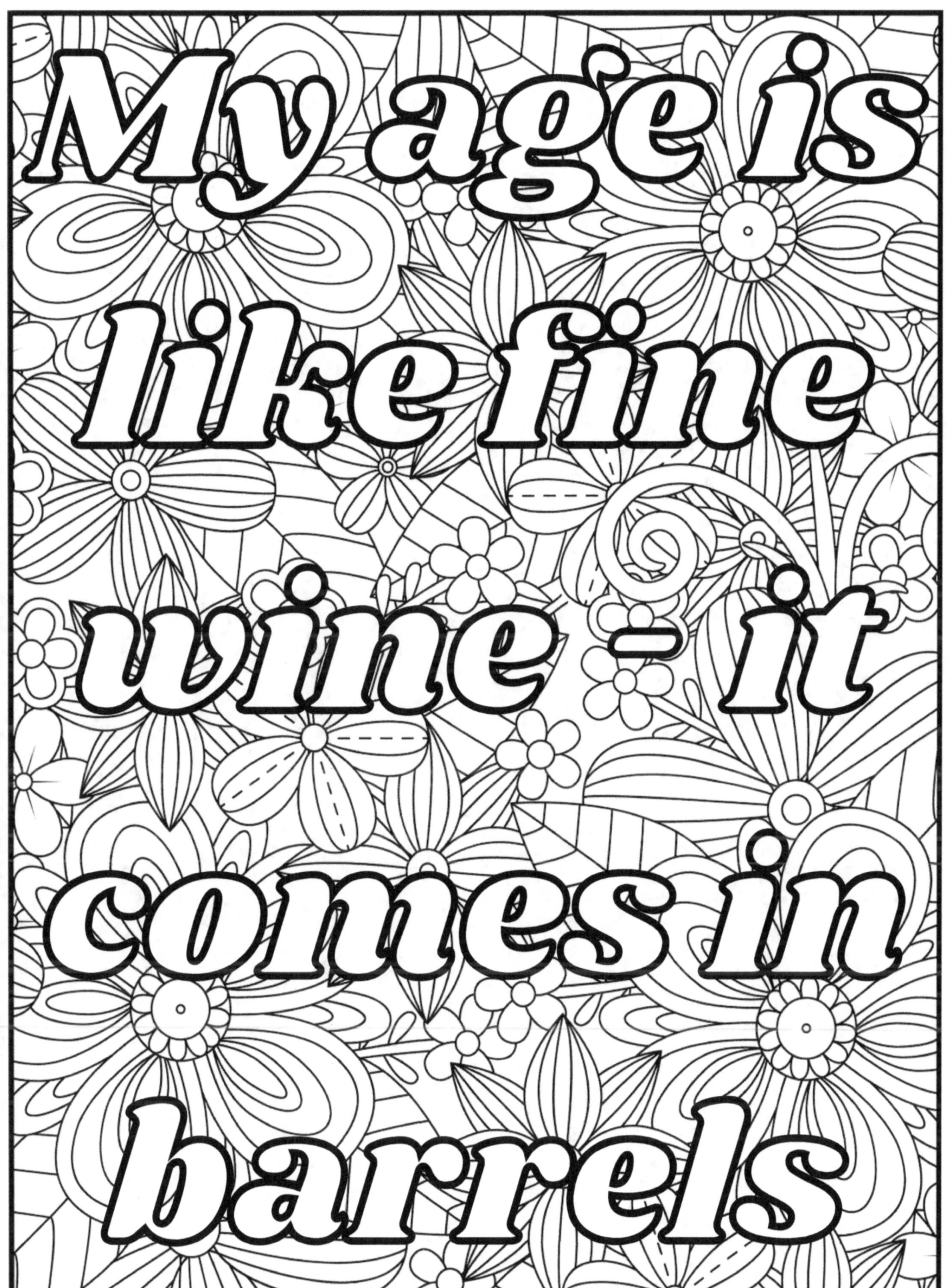

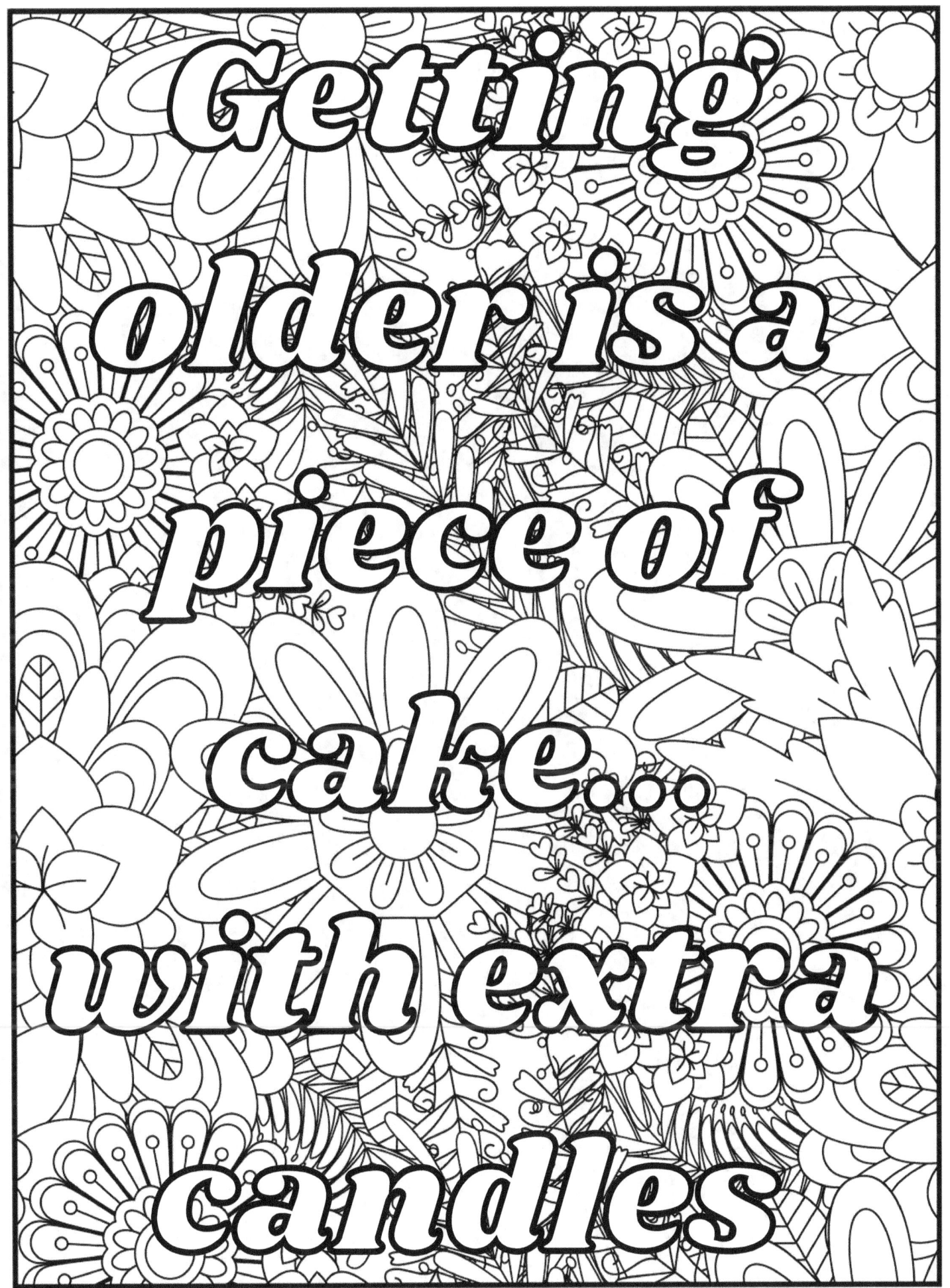

Getting older is a piece of cake... with extra candles

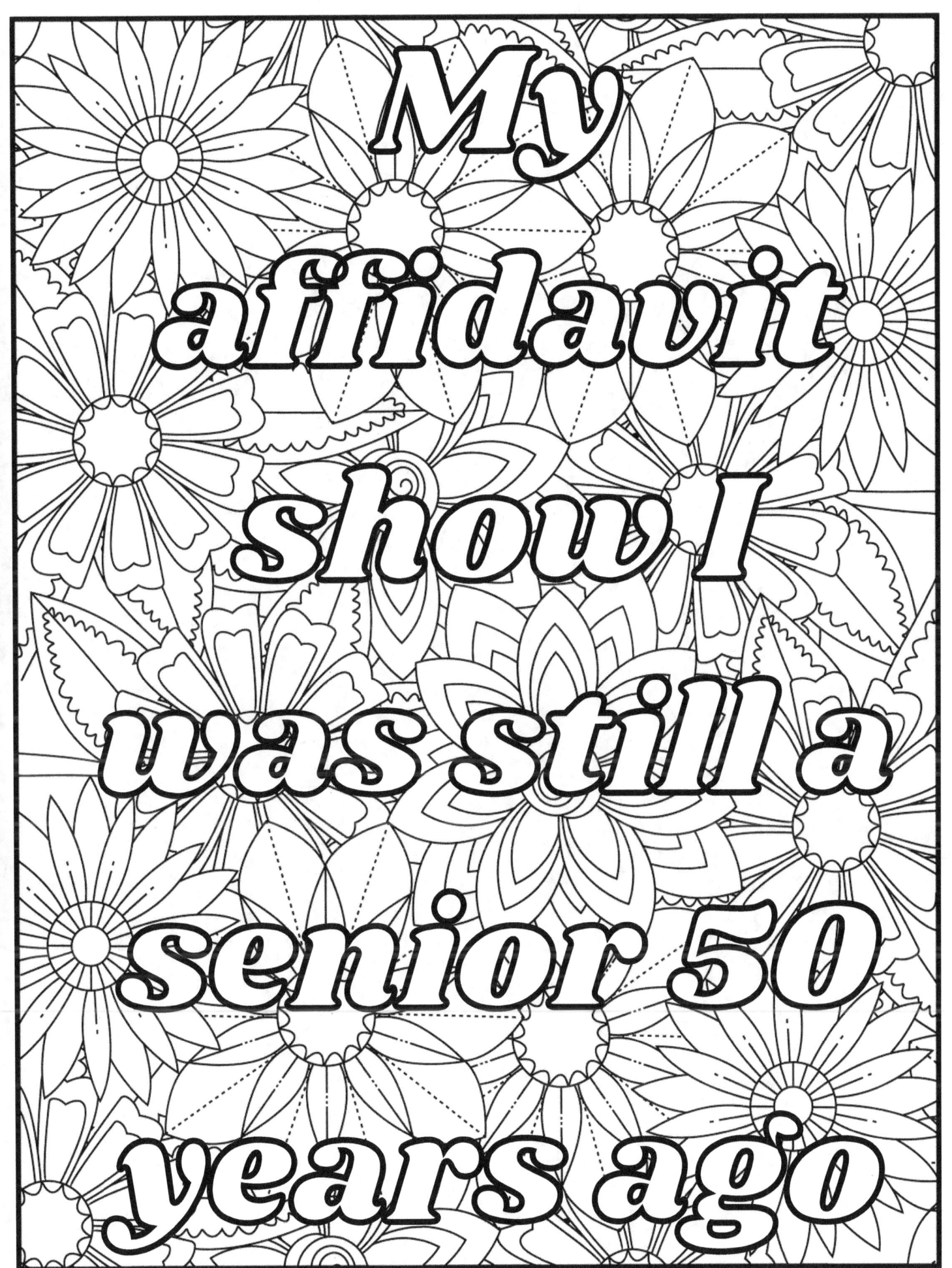

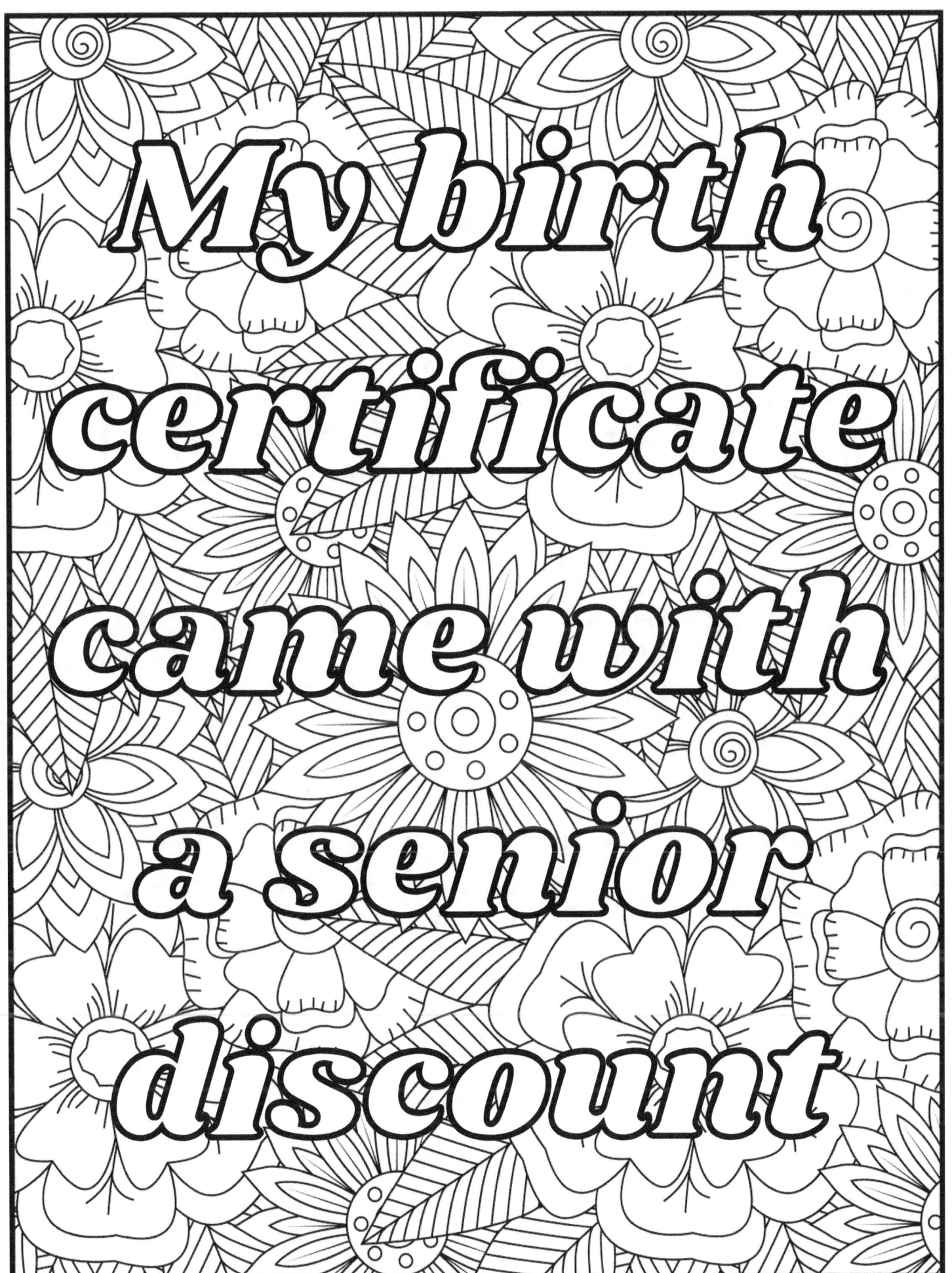

My birth certificate came with a senior discount

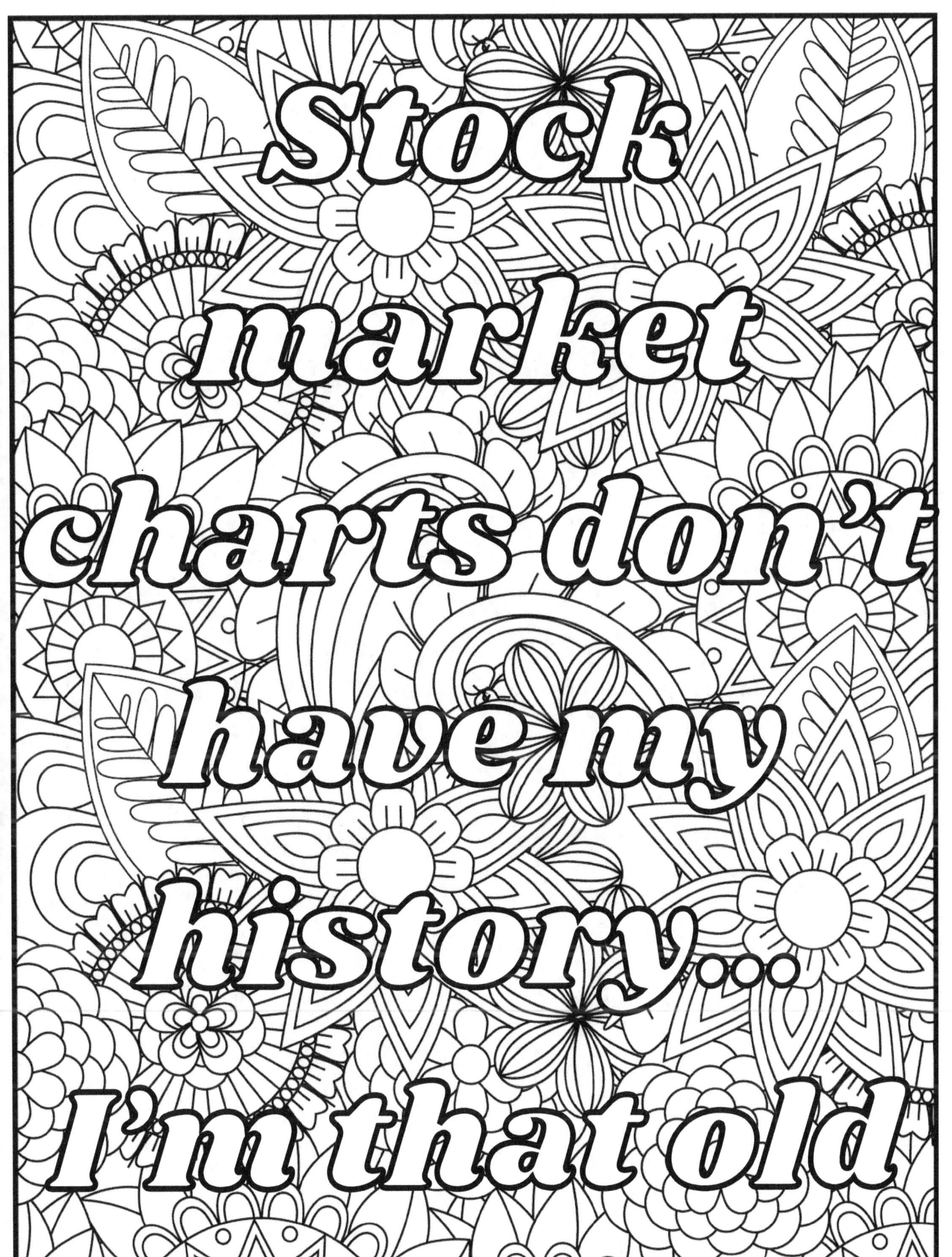

Stock market charts don't have my history.... I'm that old

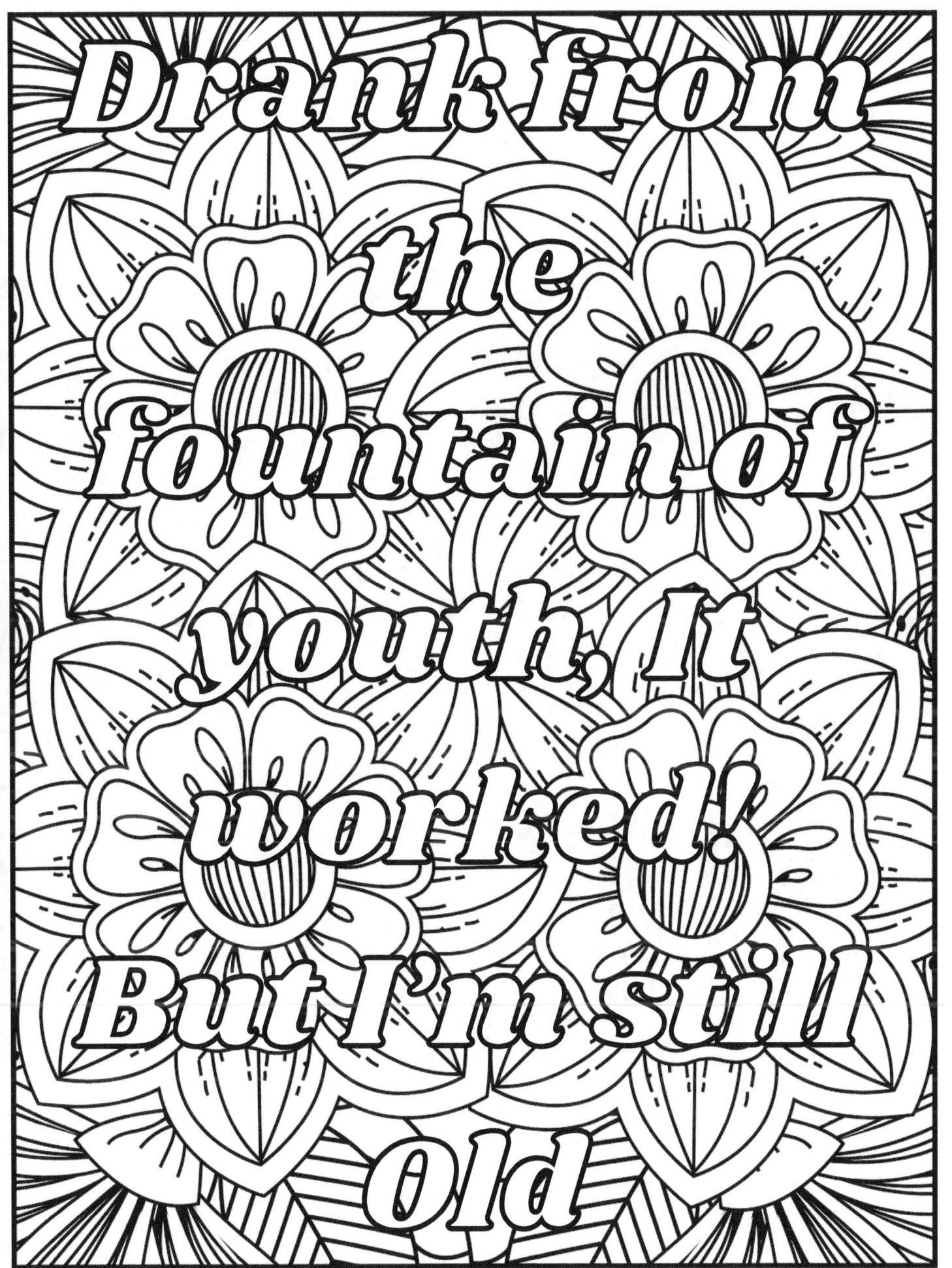

Drank from the fountain of youth, It worked! But I'm still Old

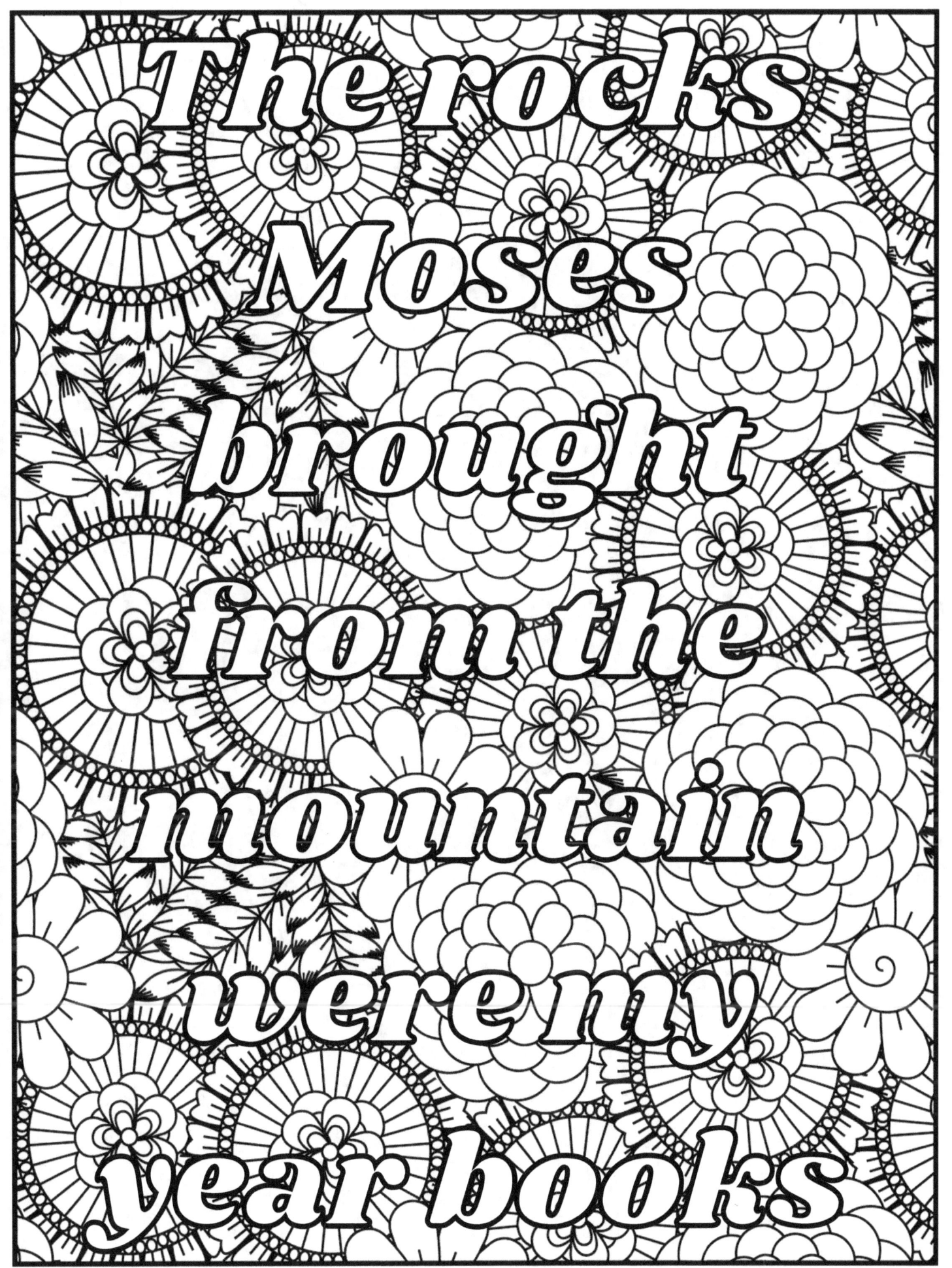

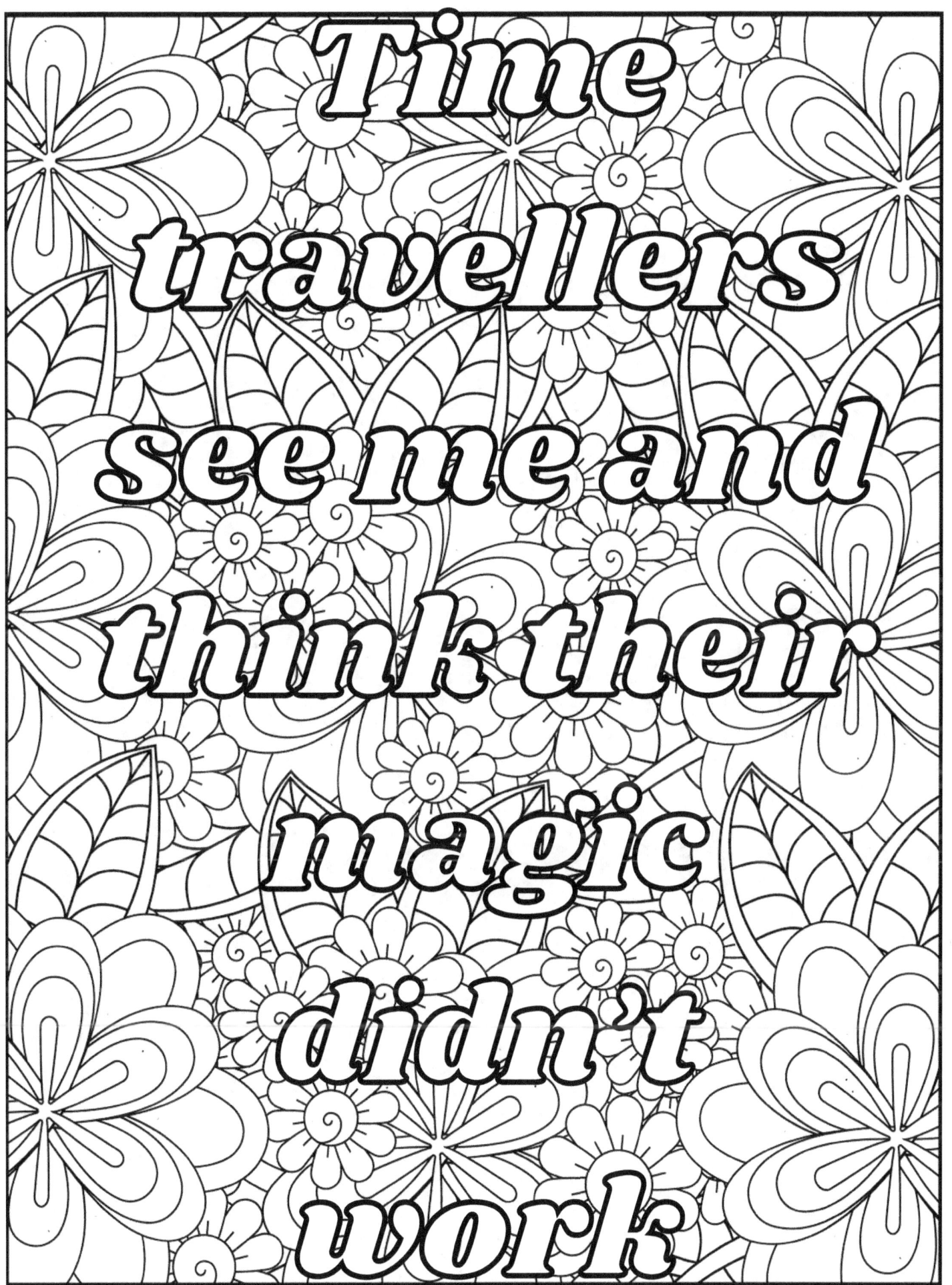

Time travellers see me and think their magic didn't work

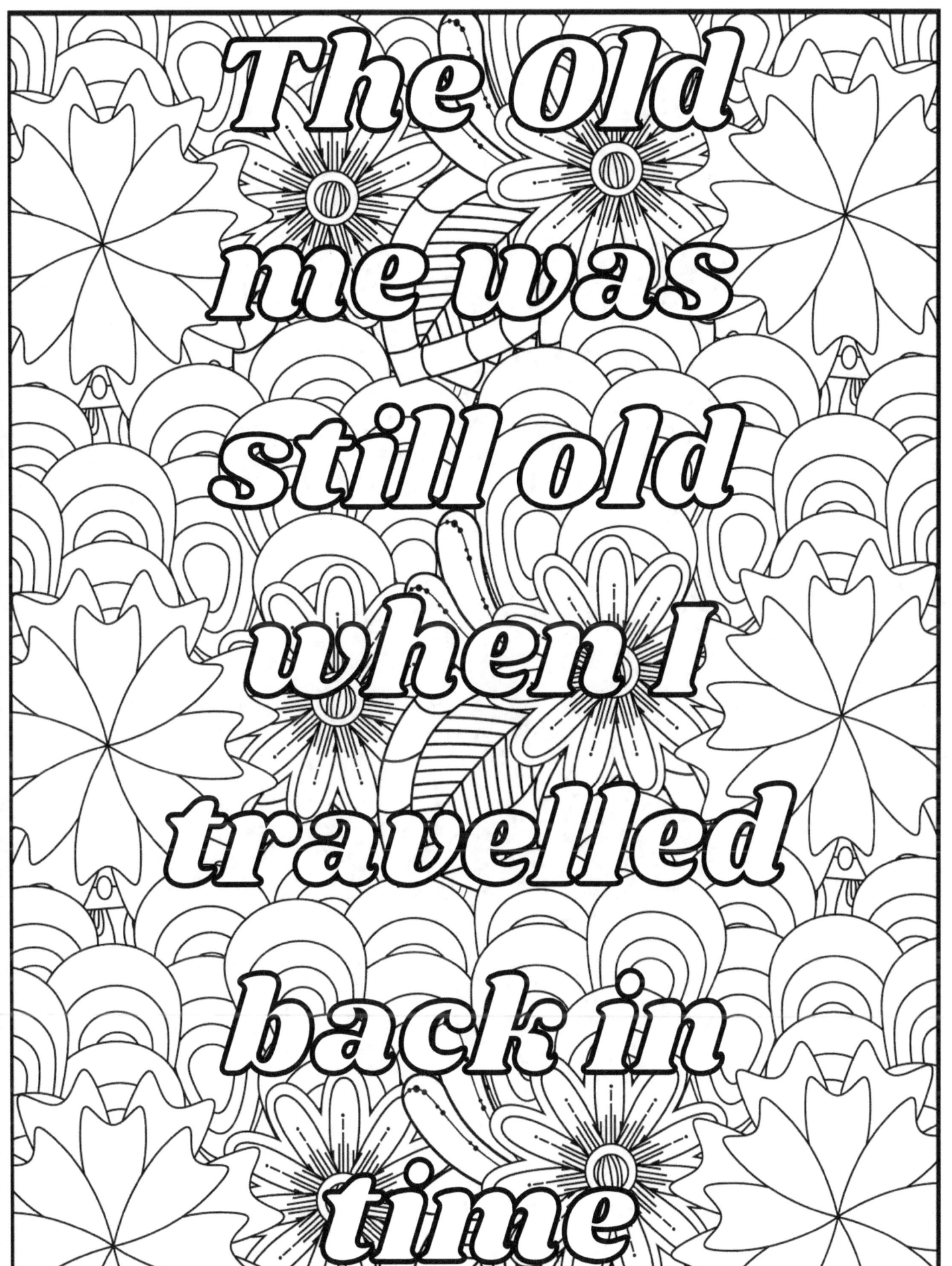

The Old me was still old when I travelled back in time

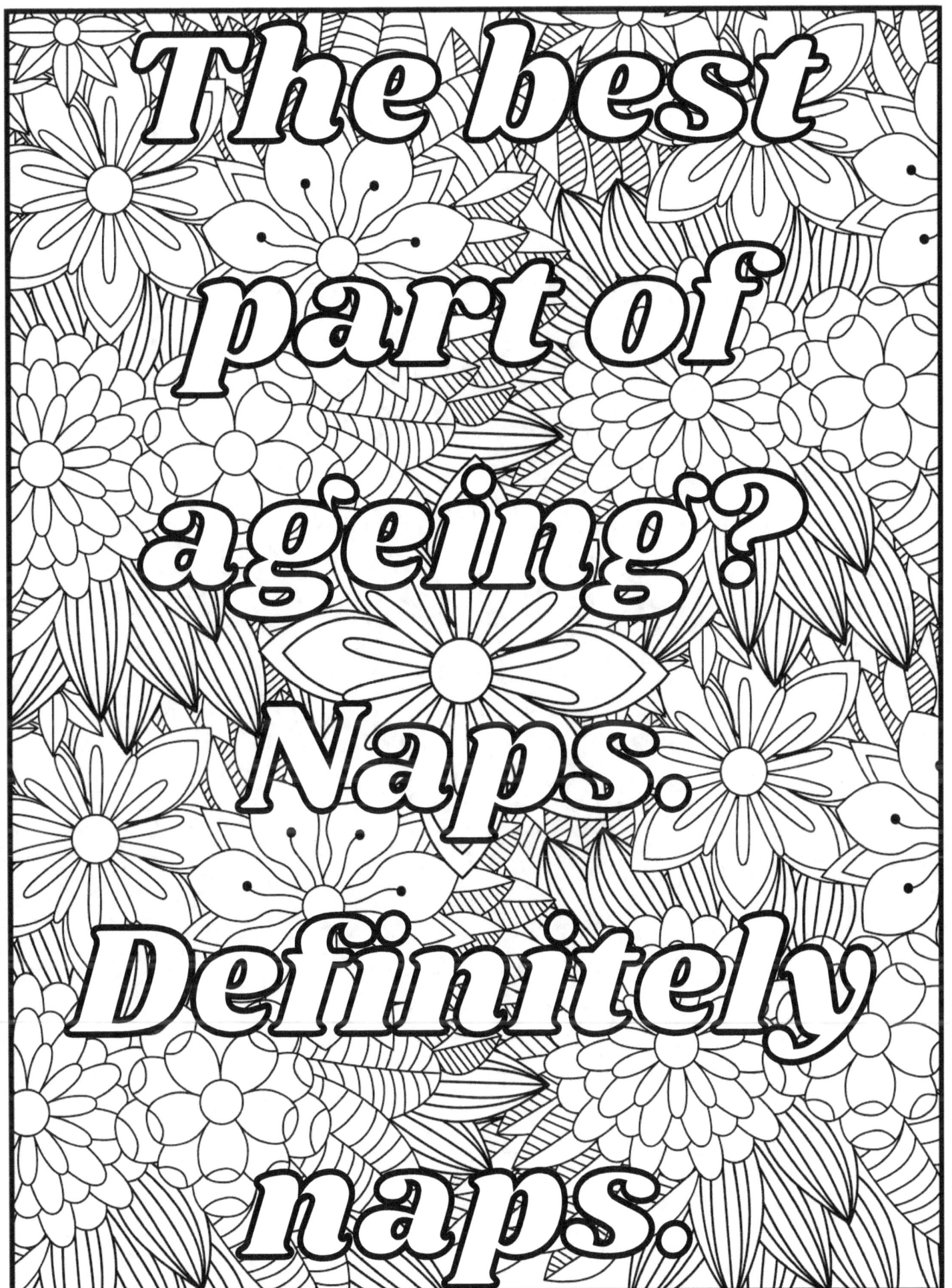

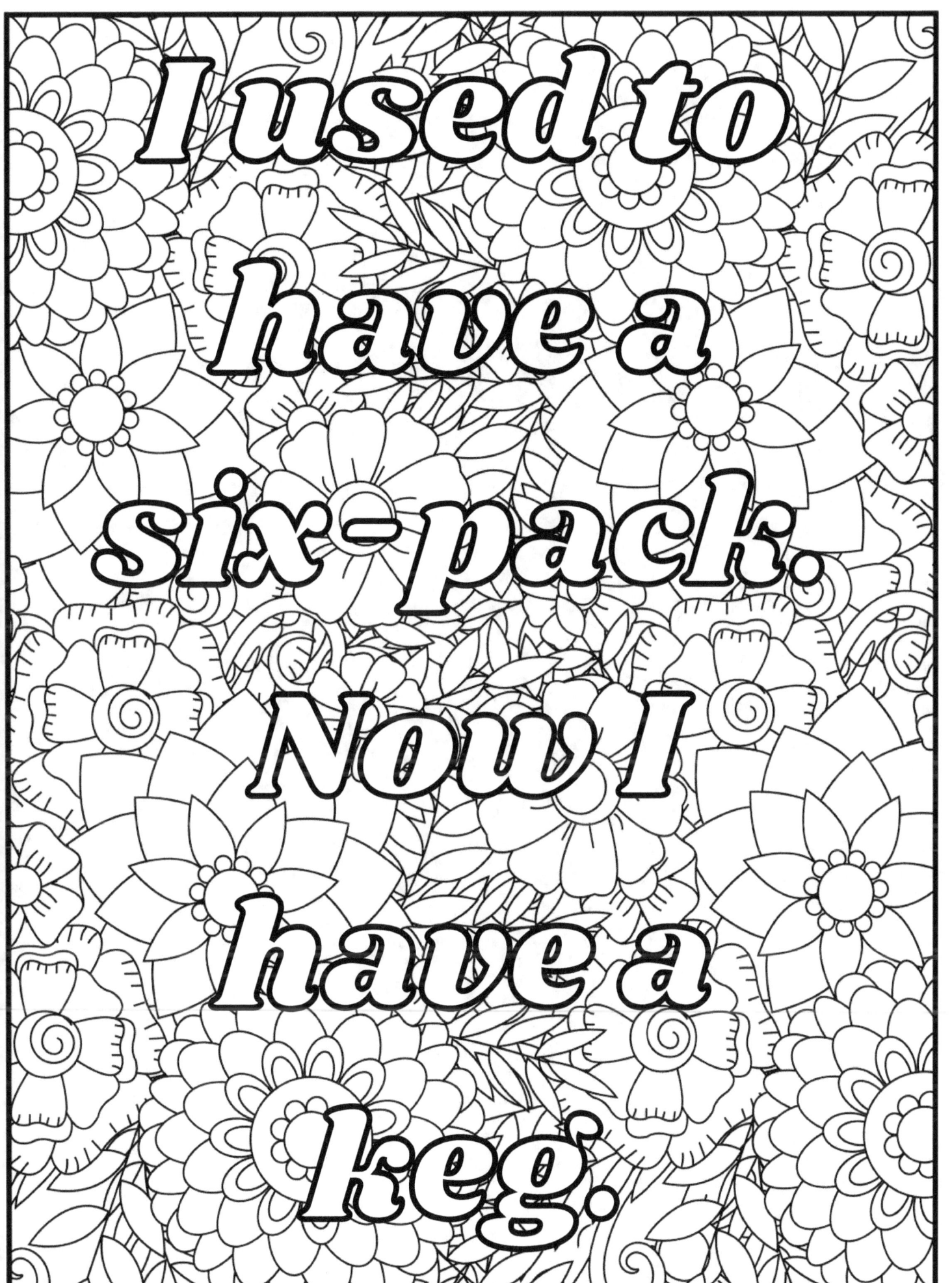

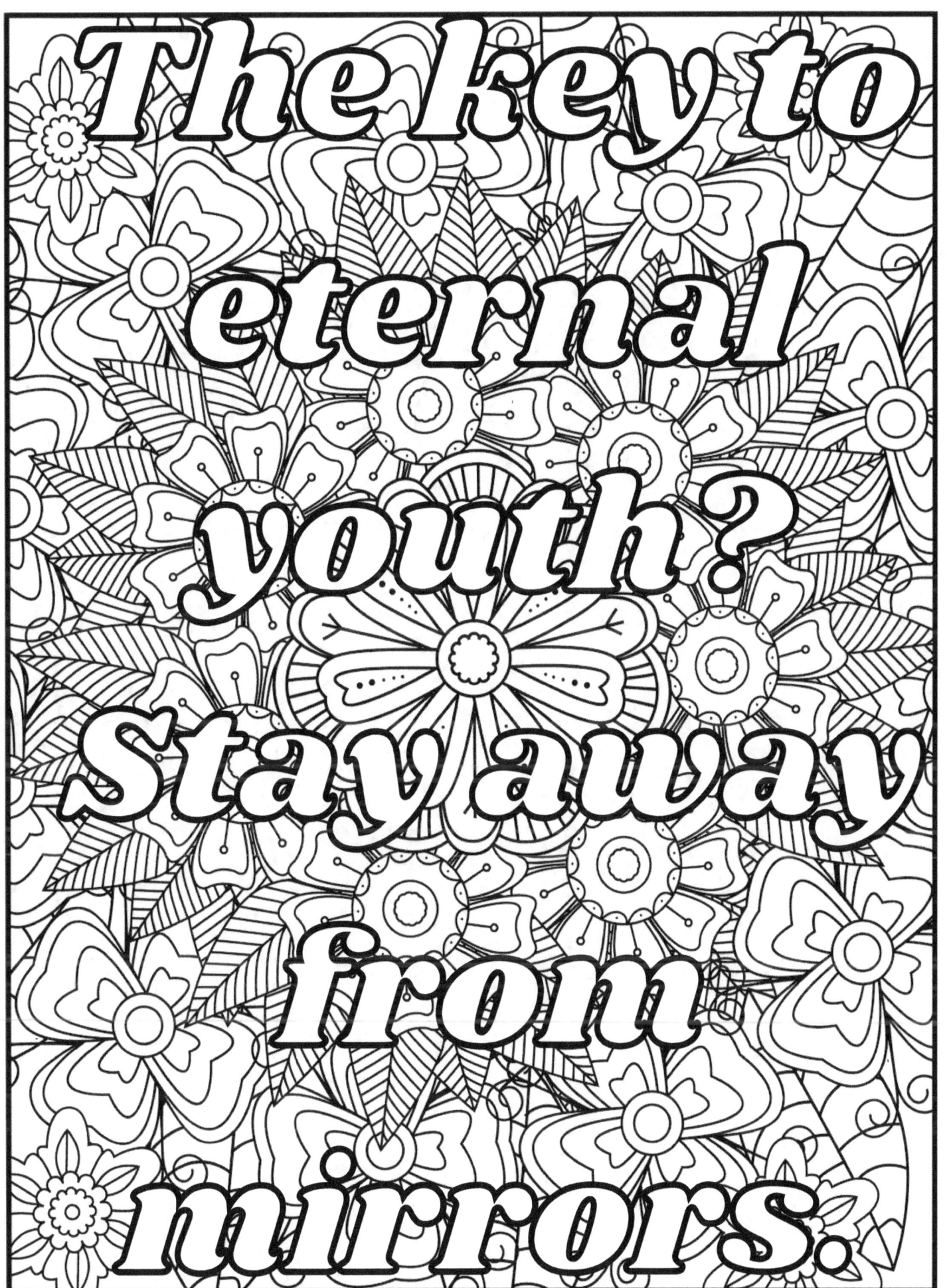

The key to eternal youth? Stay away from mirrors.

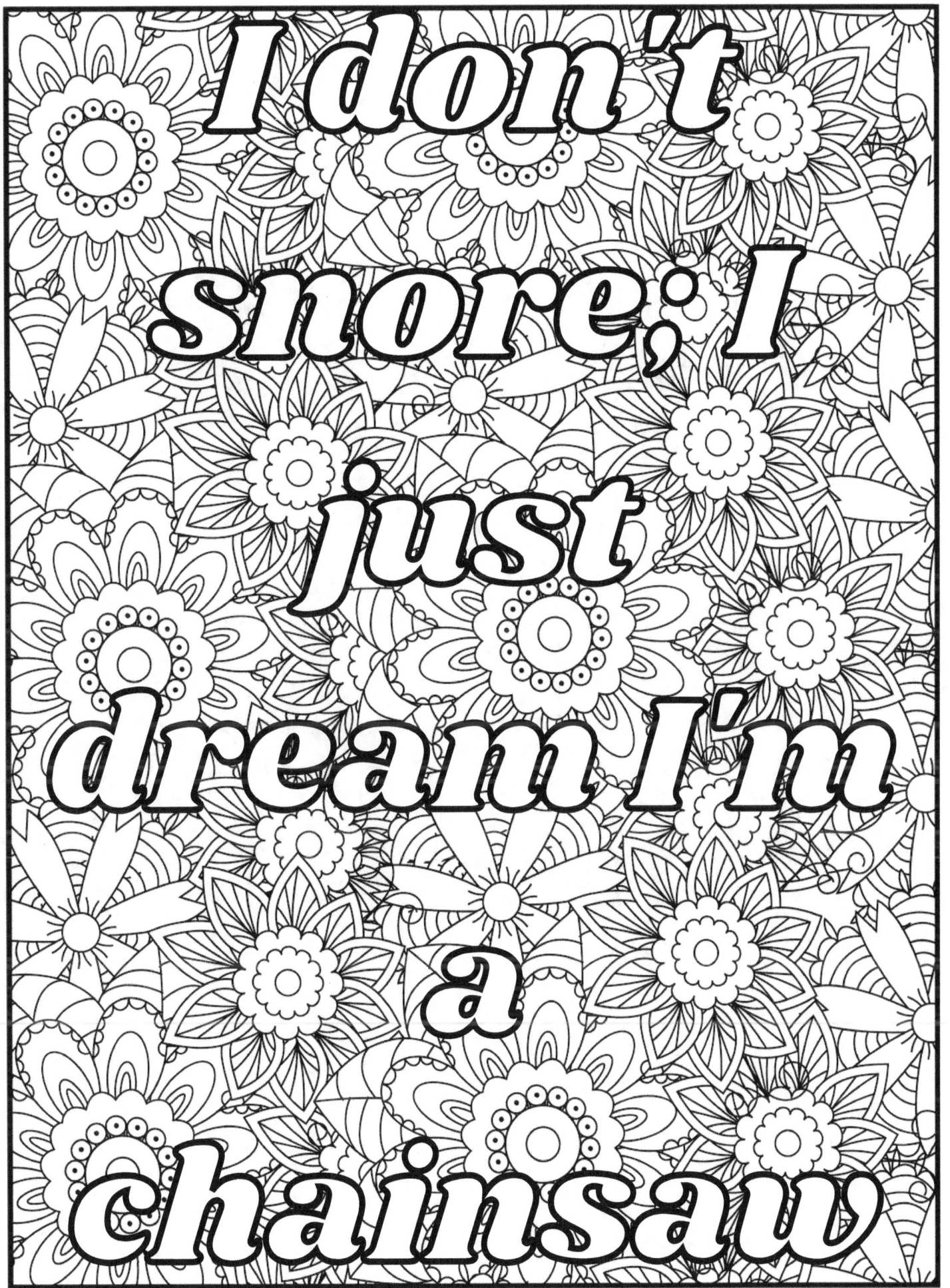

I've been eligible for Senior discount for the longest time

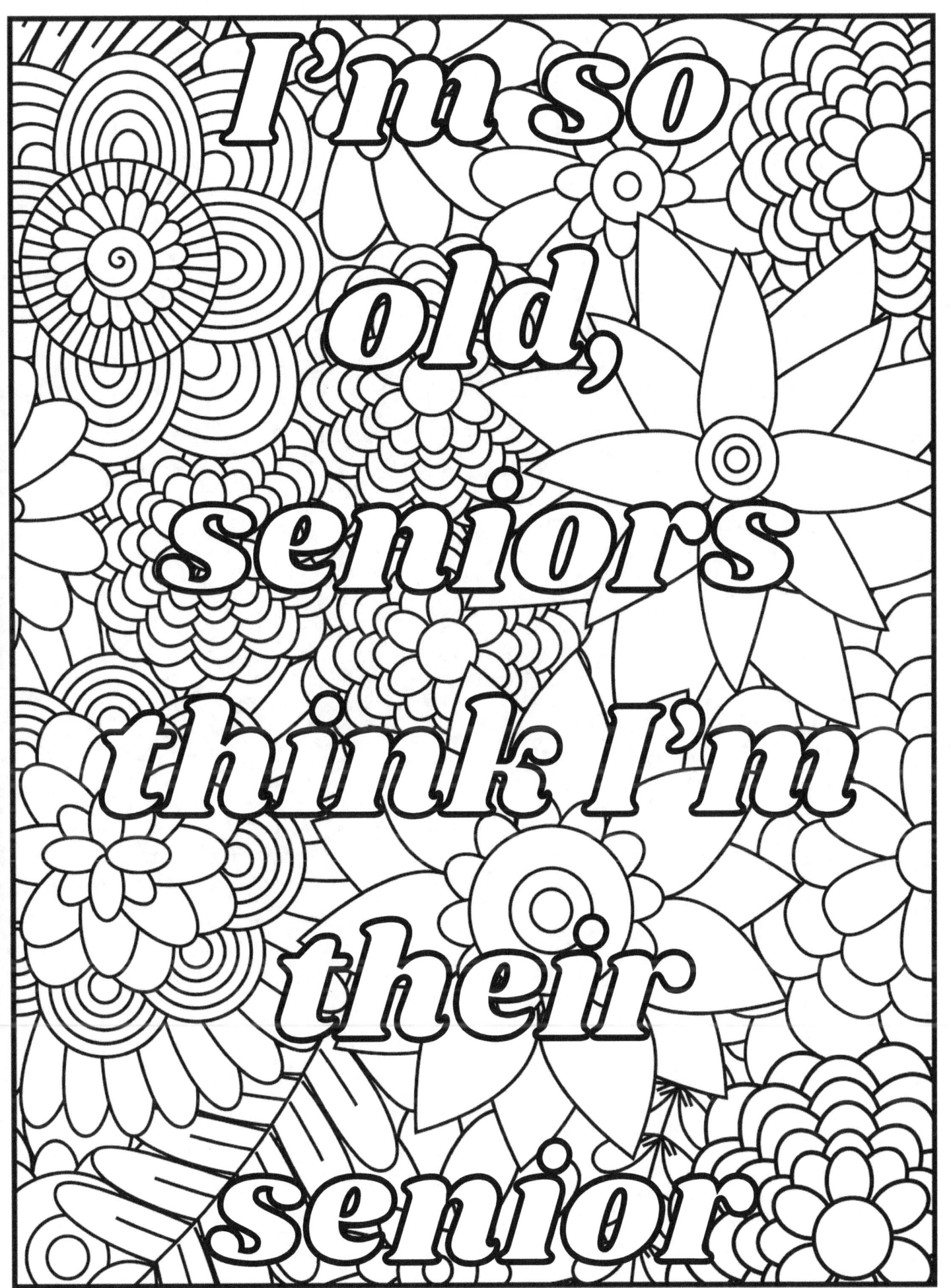

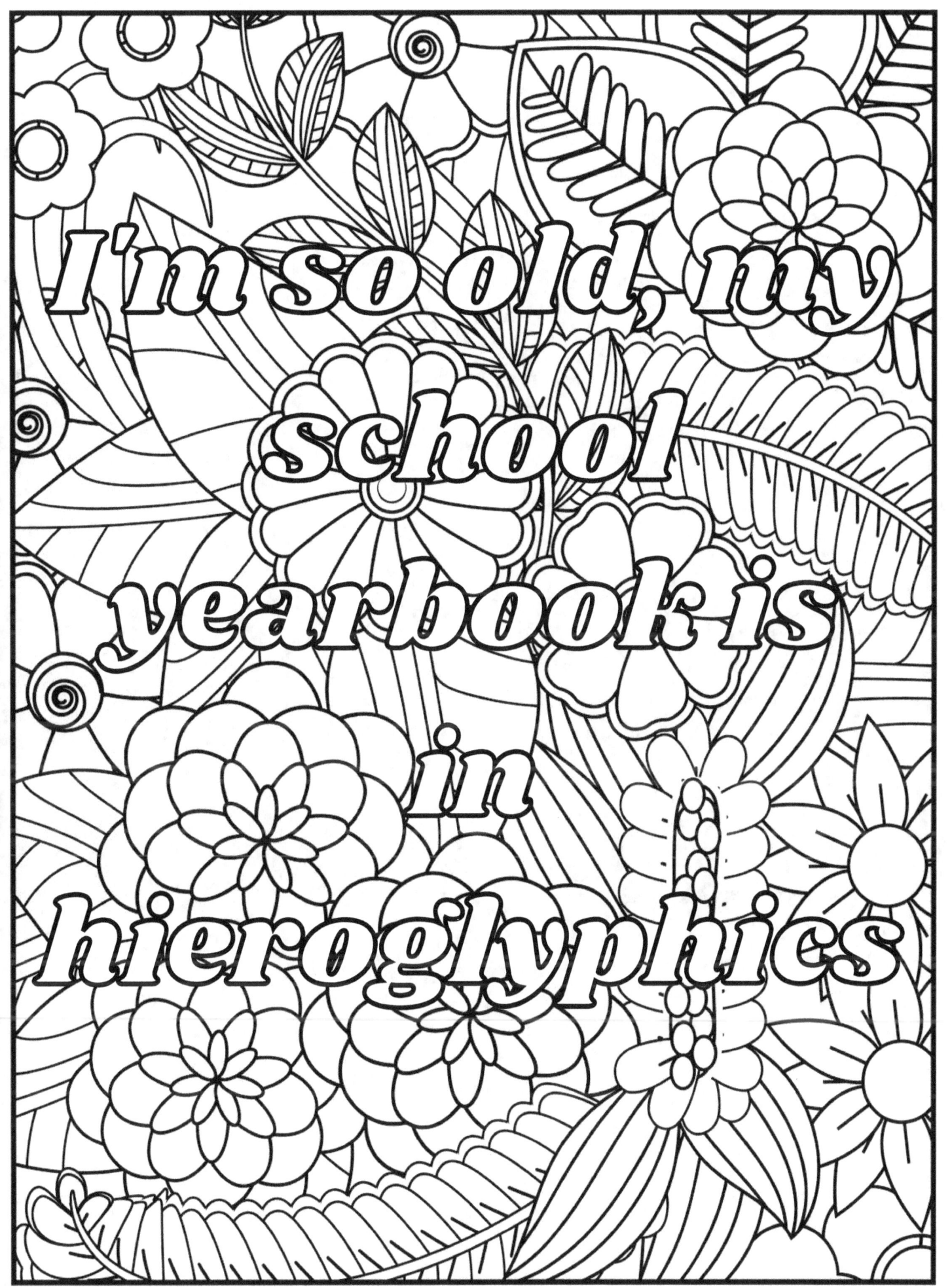

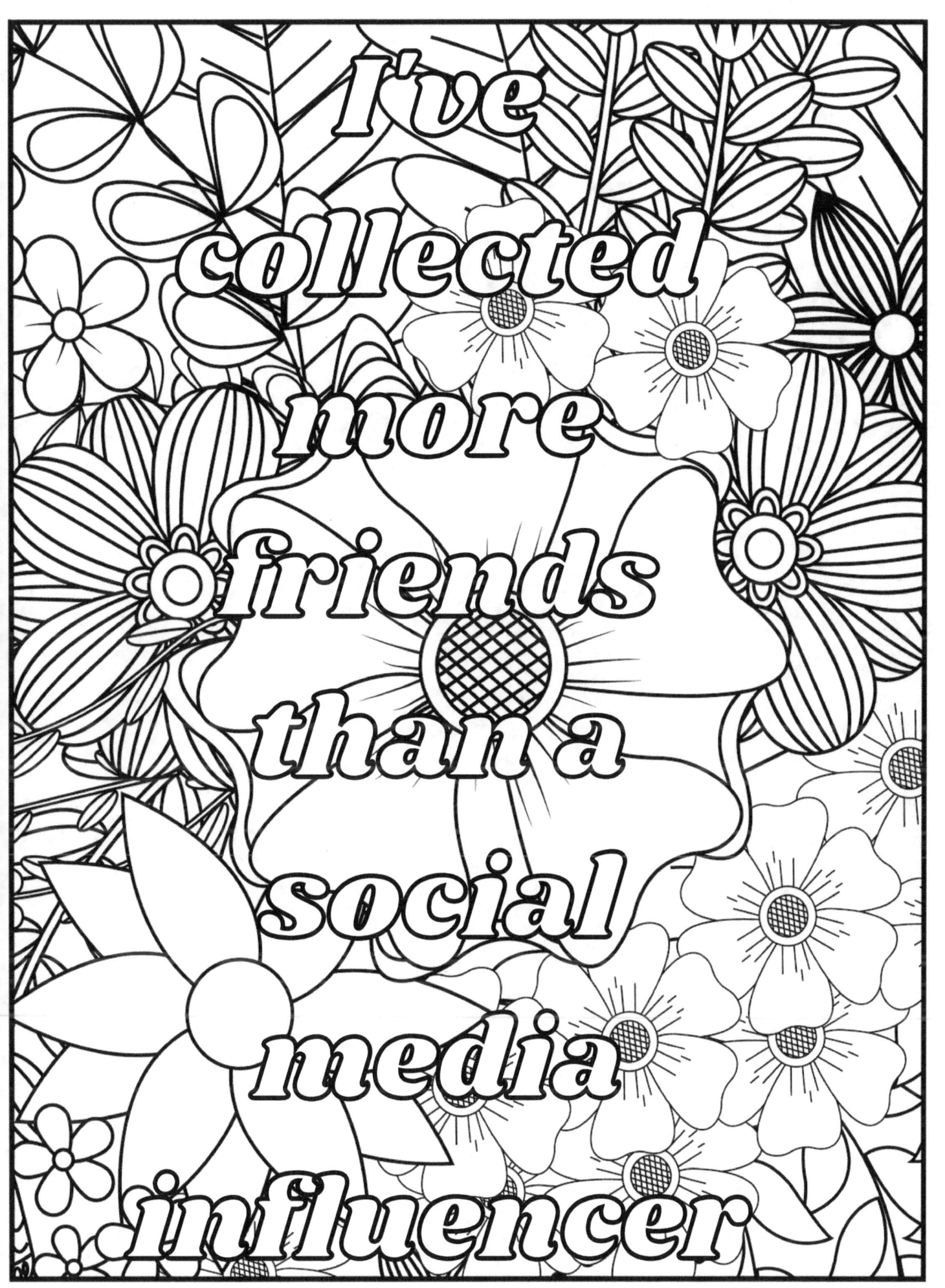

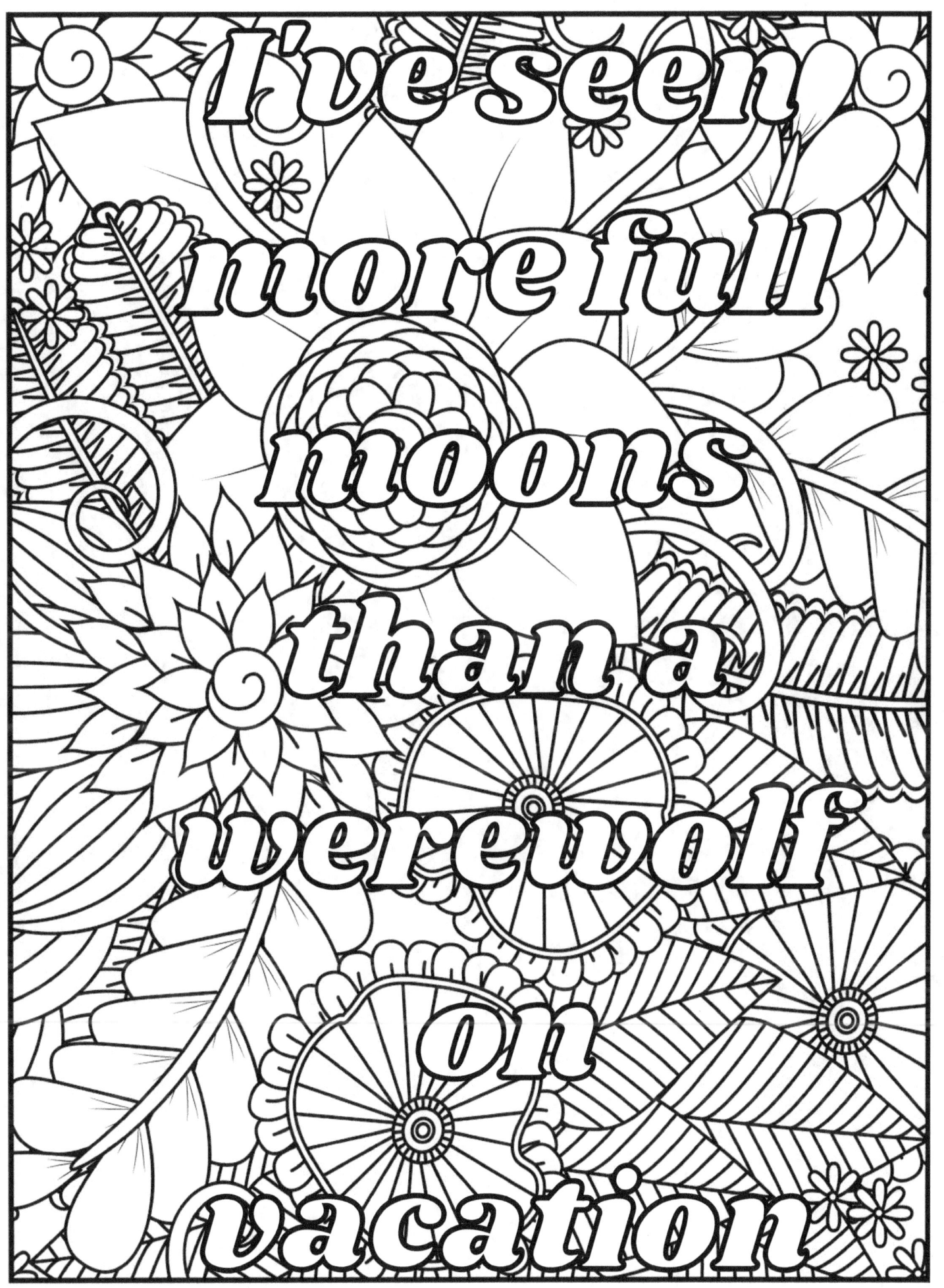

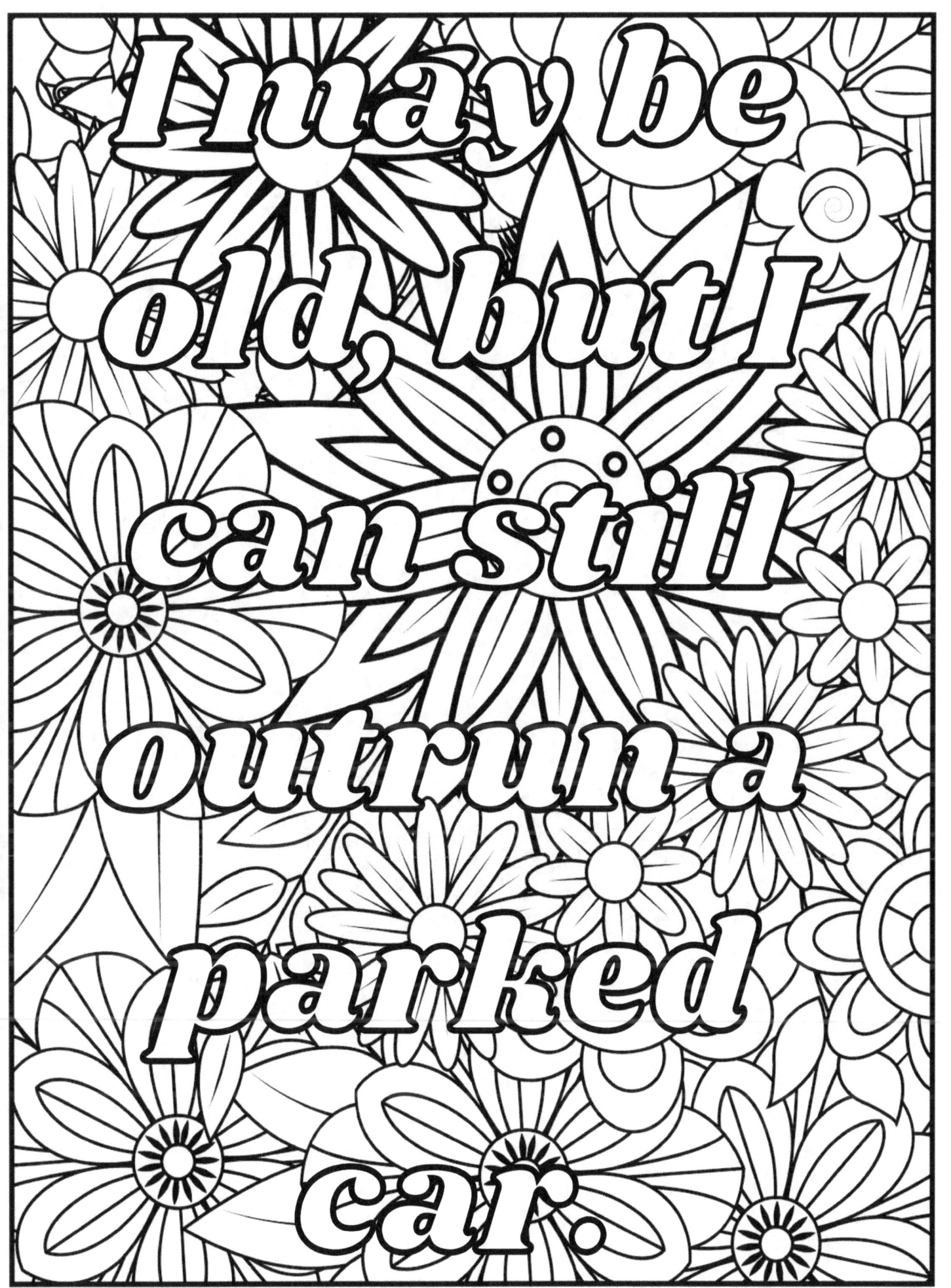

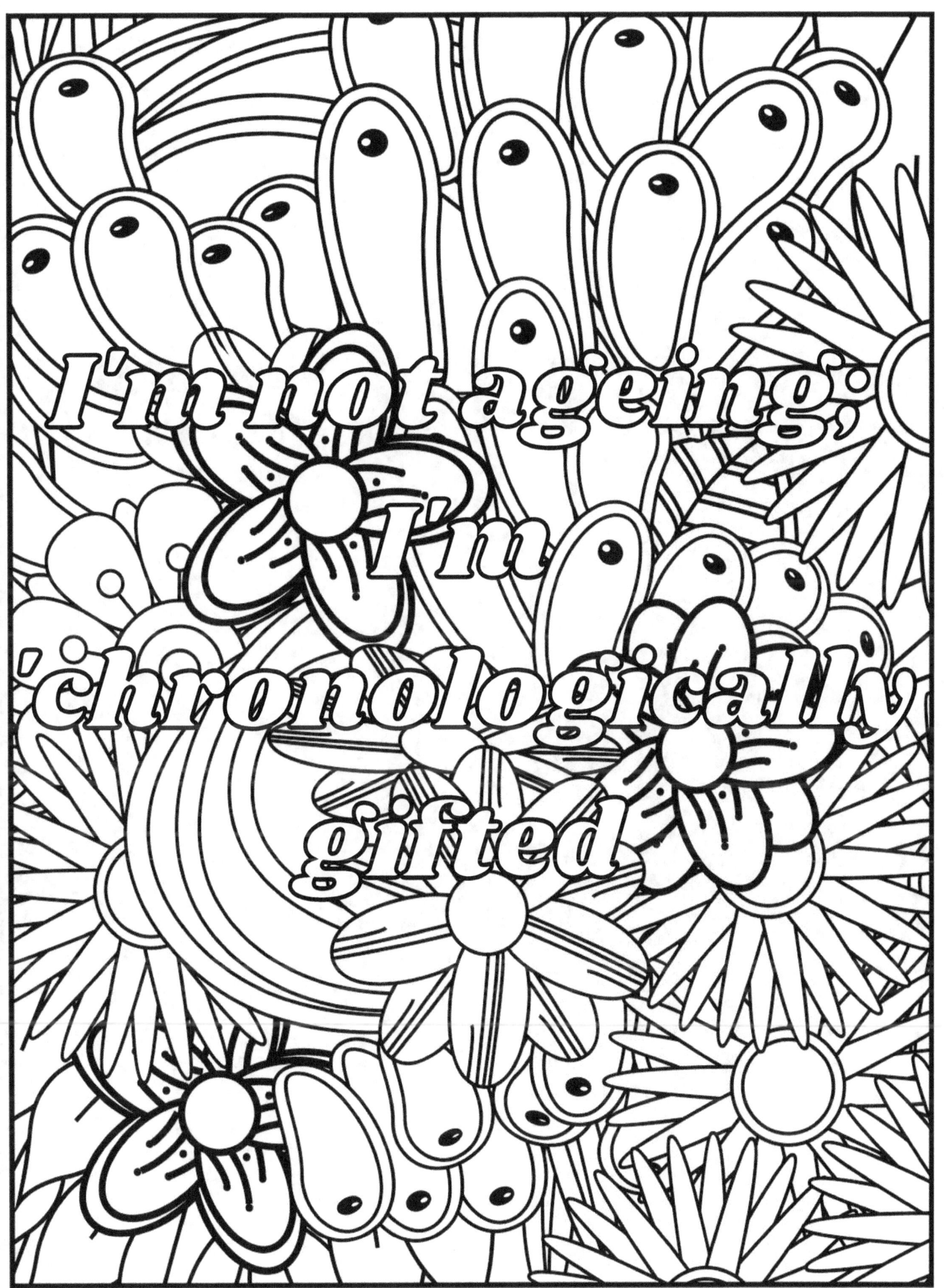

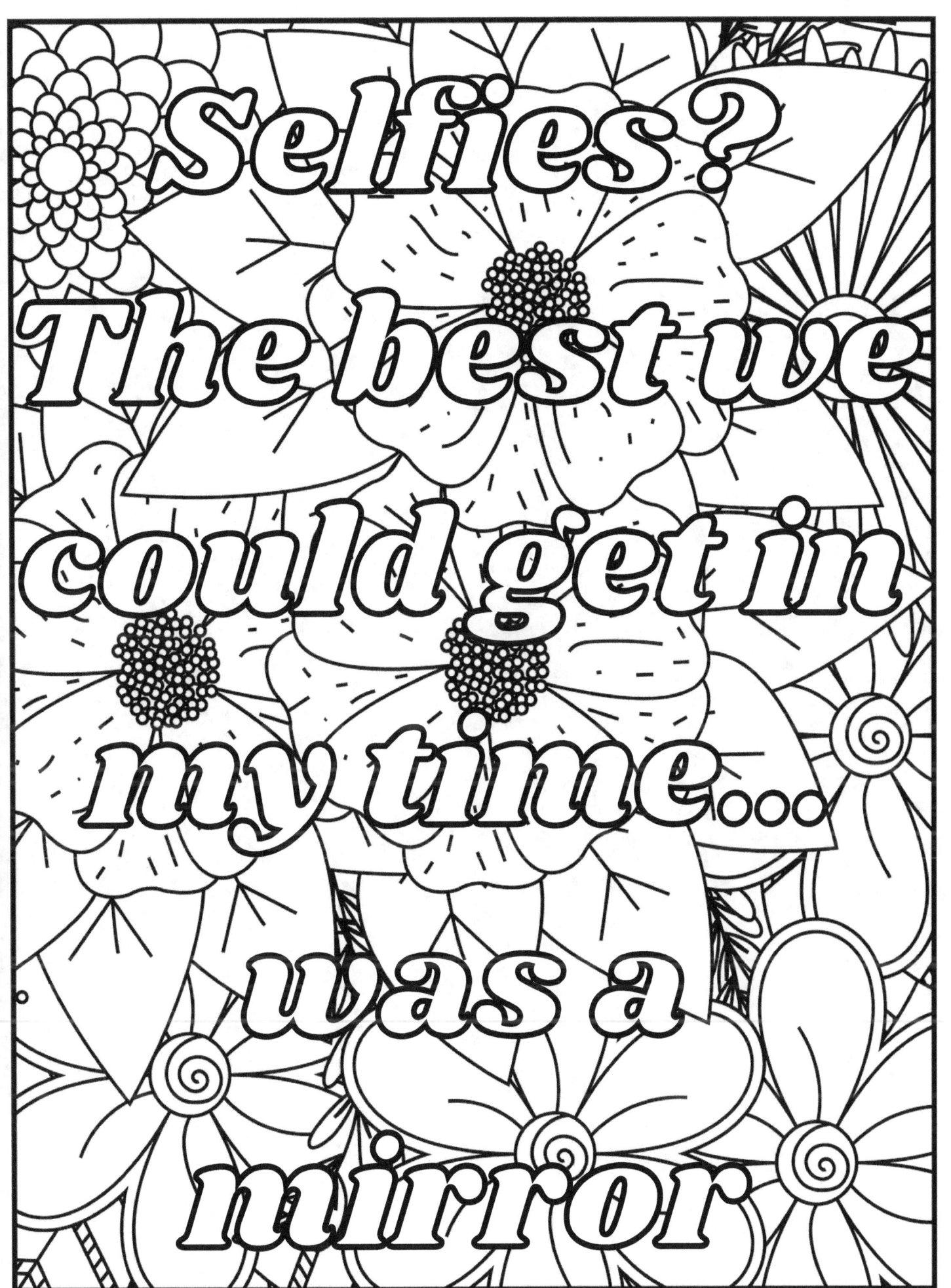

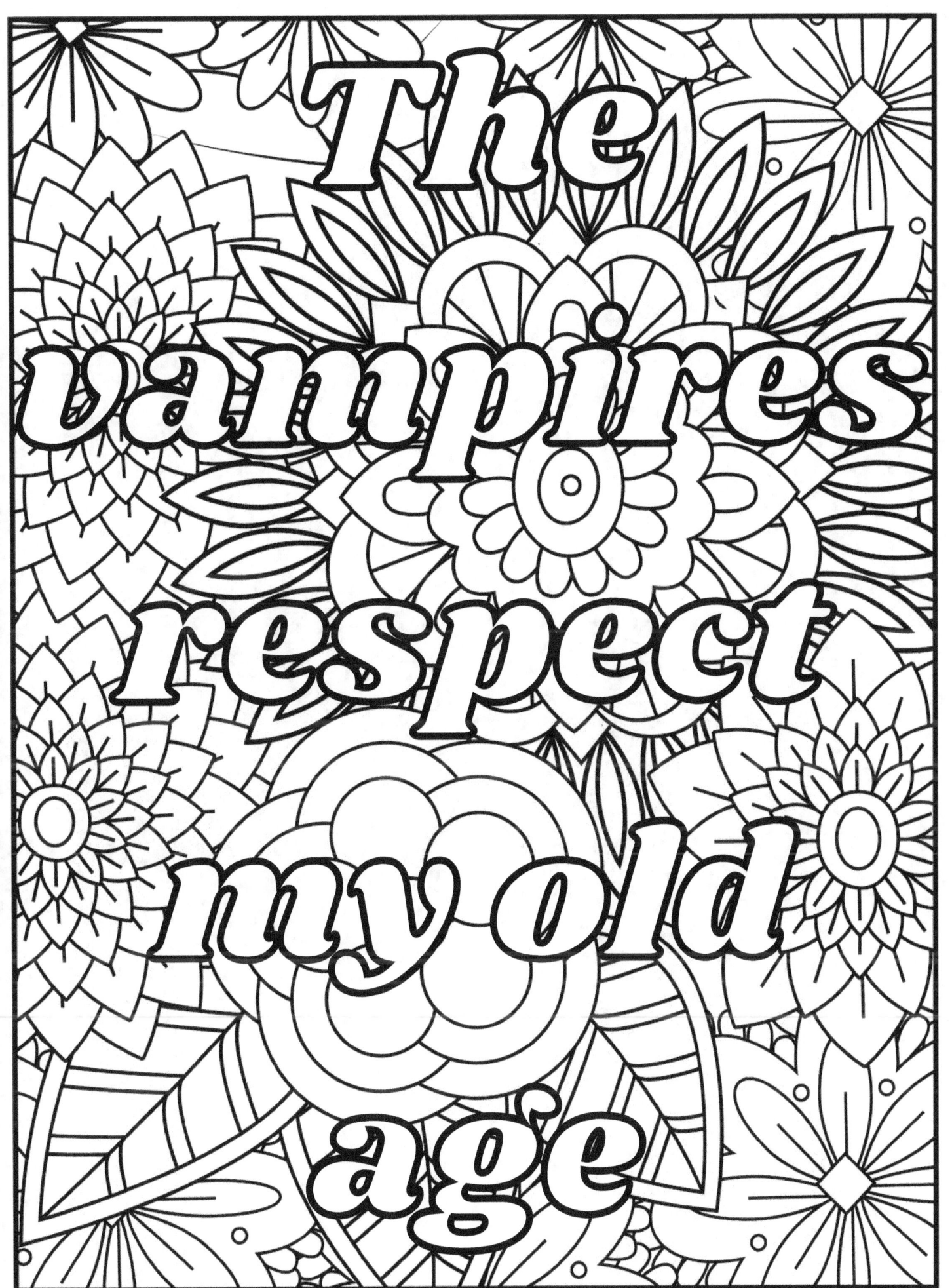

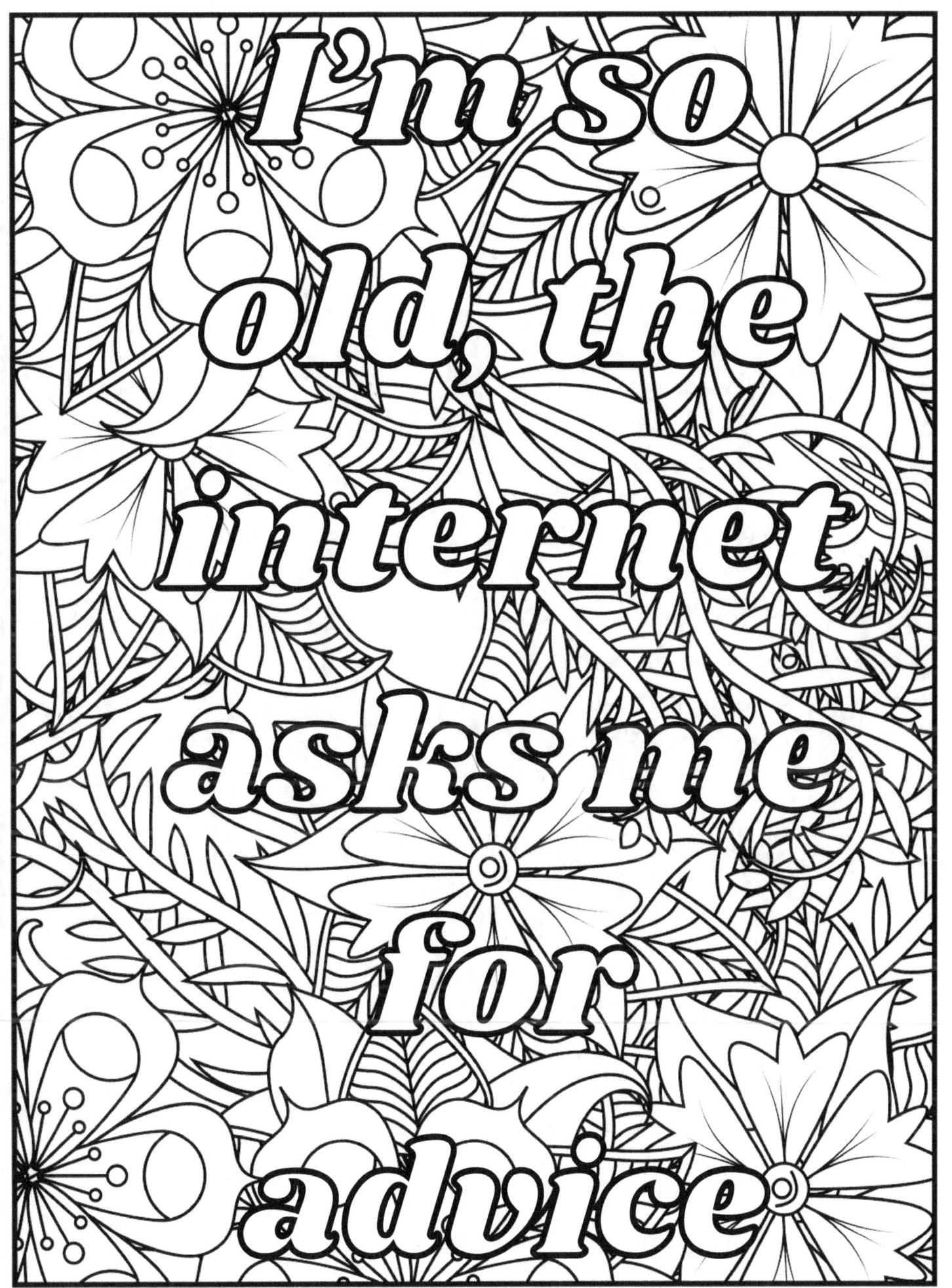

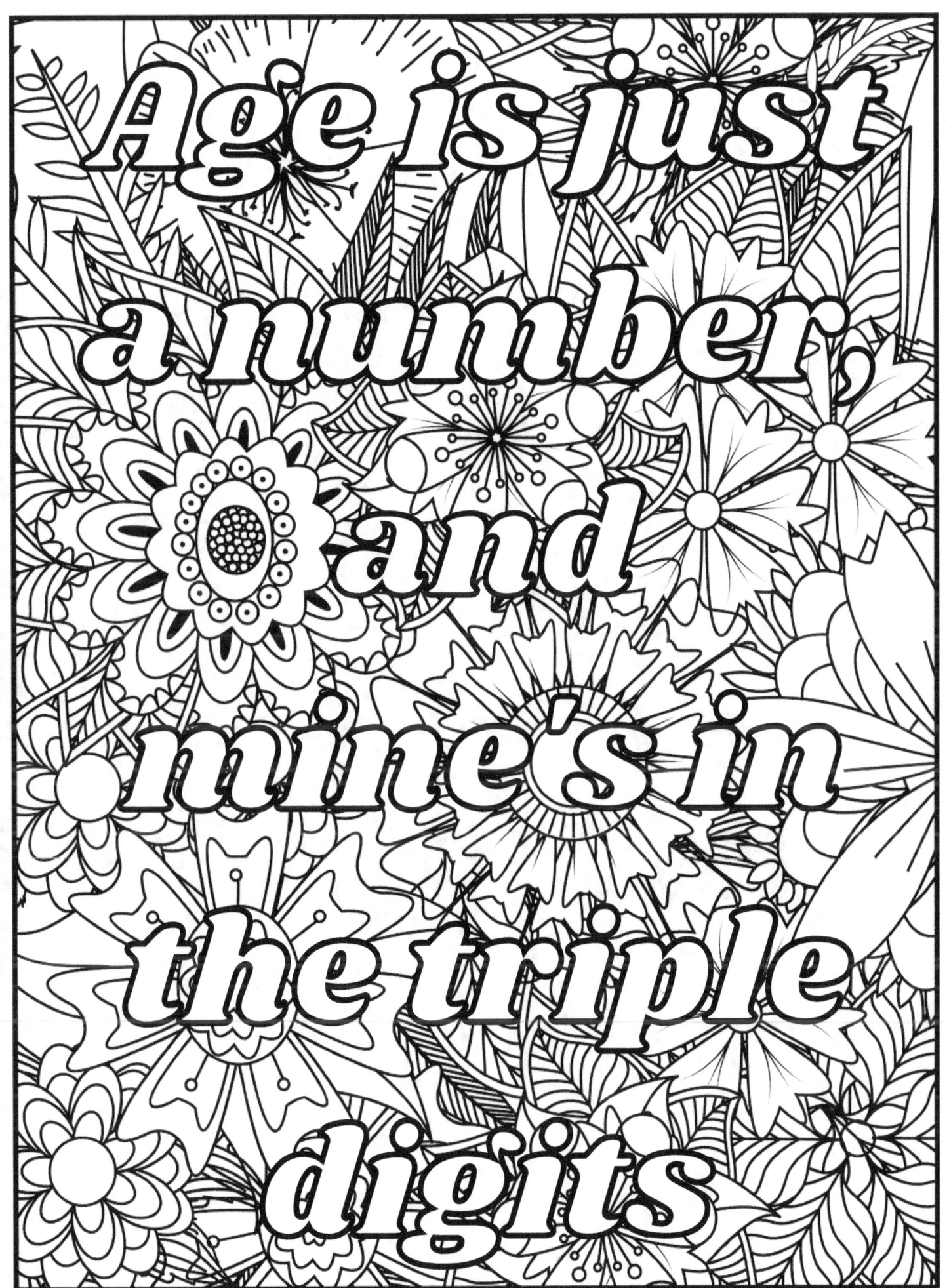

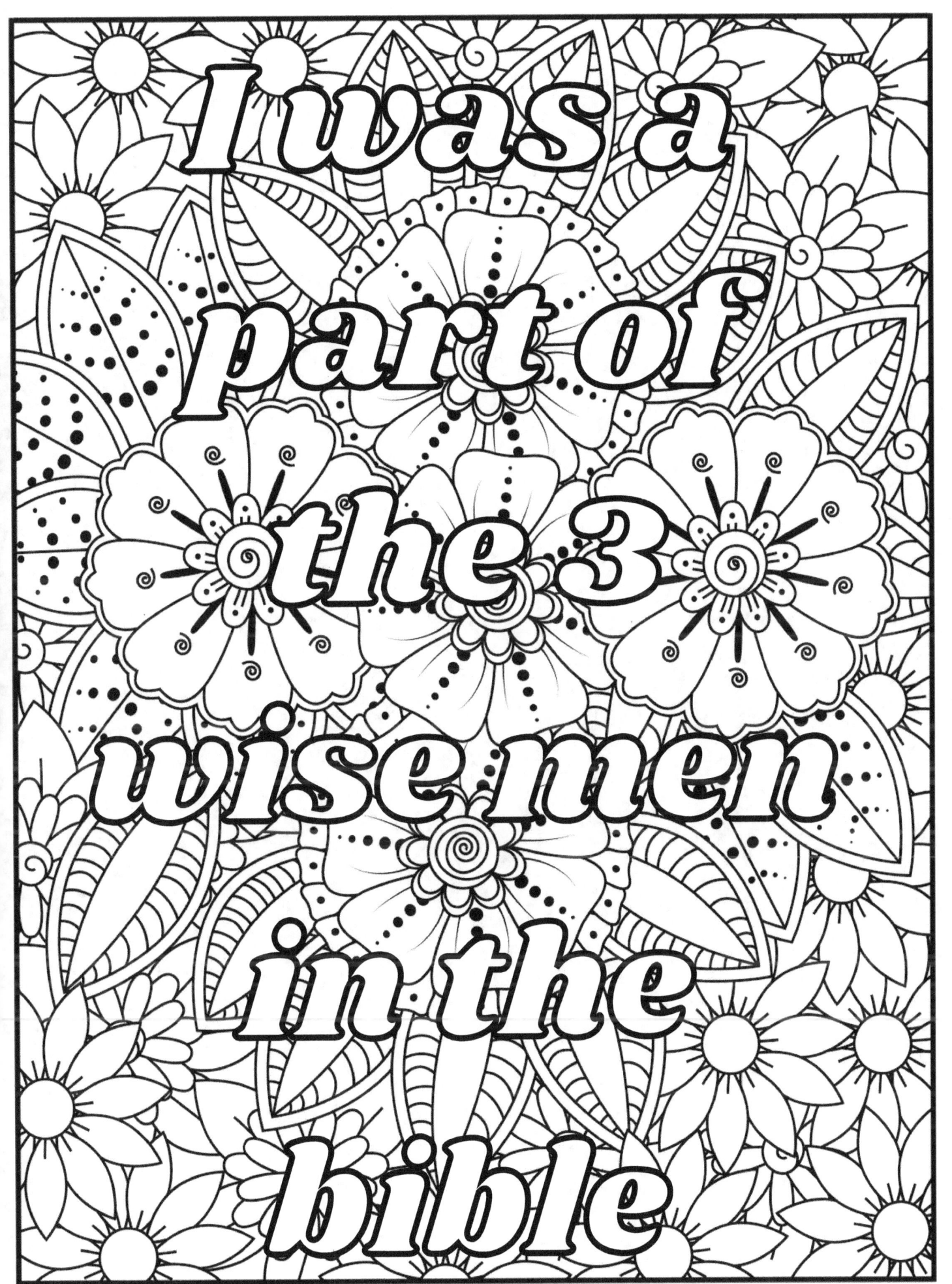

I was a part of the 3 wise men in the bible

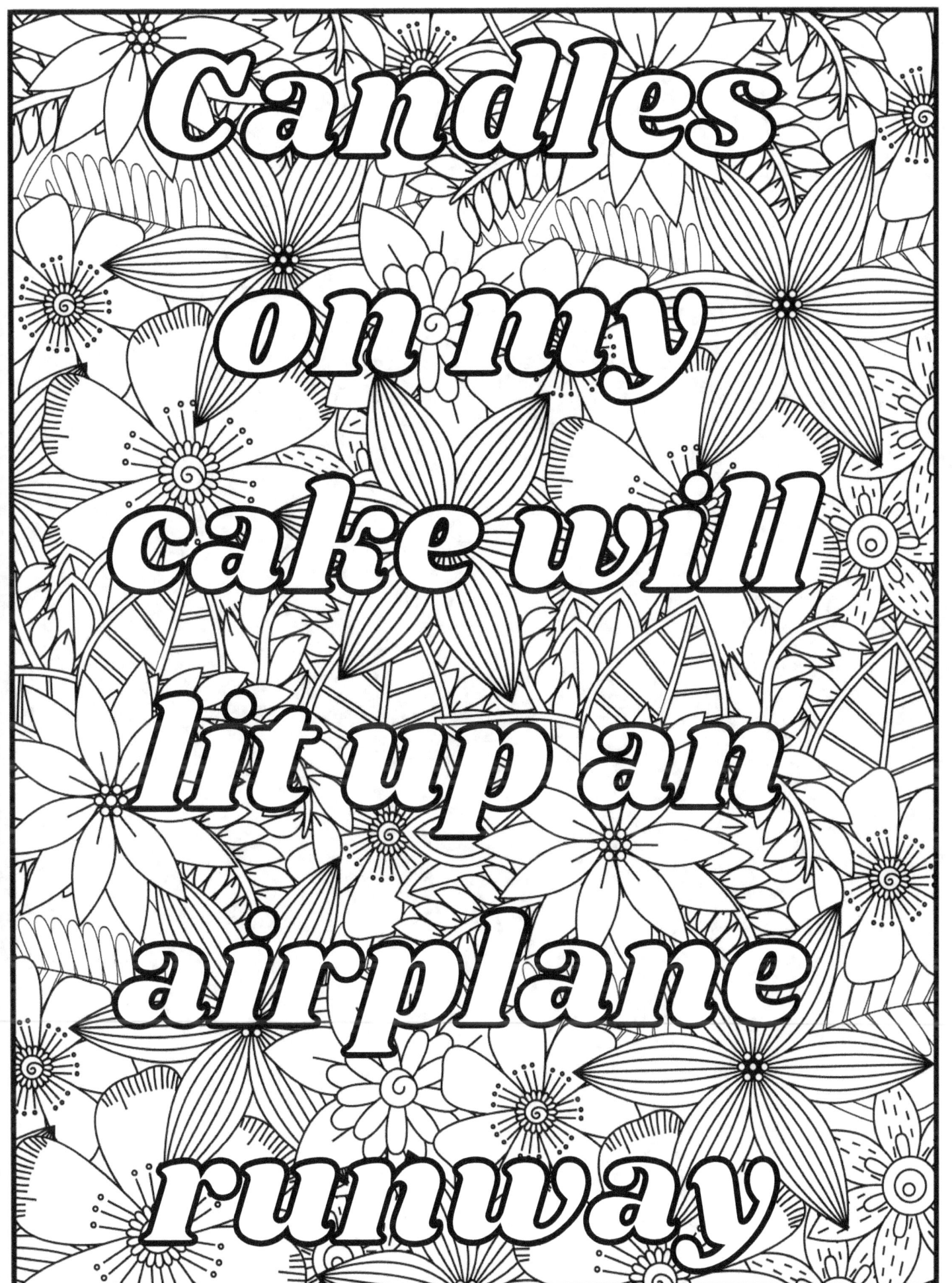

Candles on my cake will lit up an airplane runway

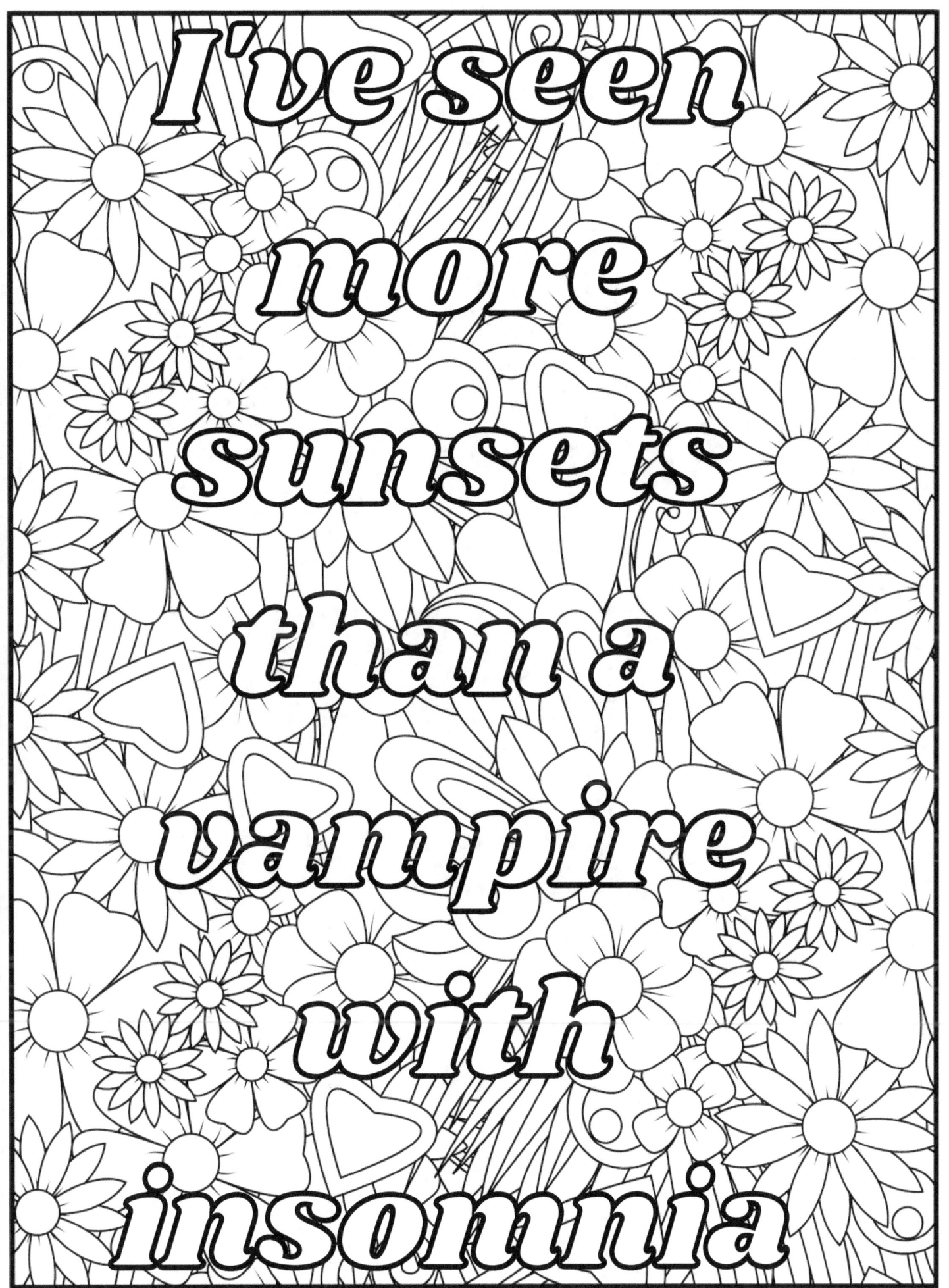

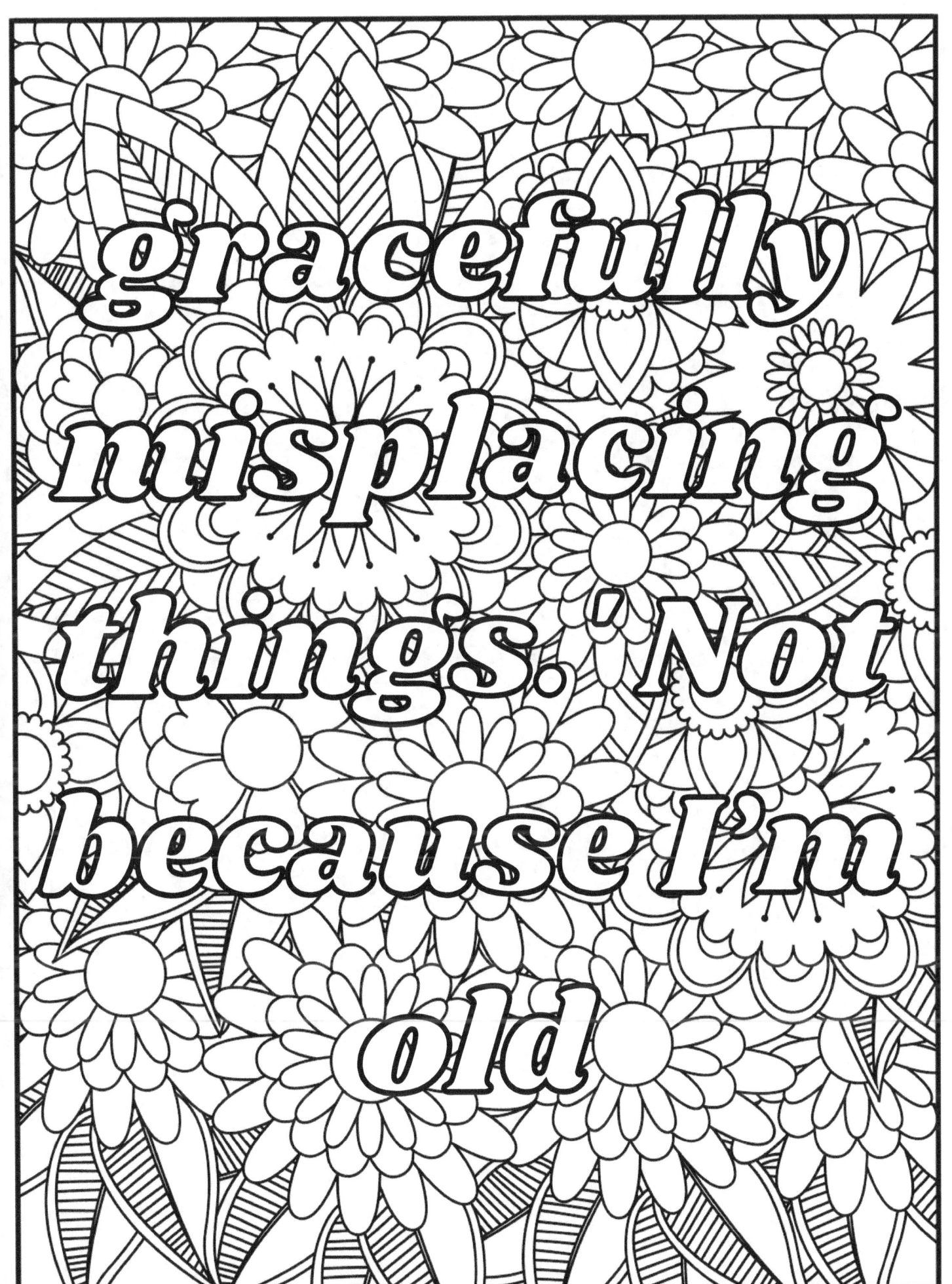

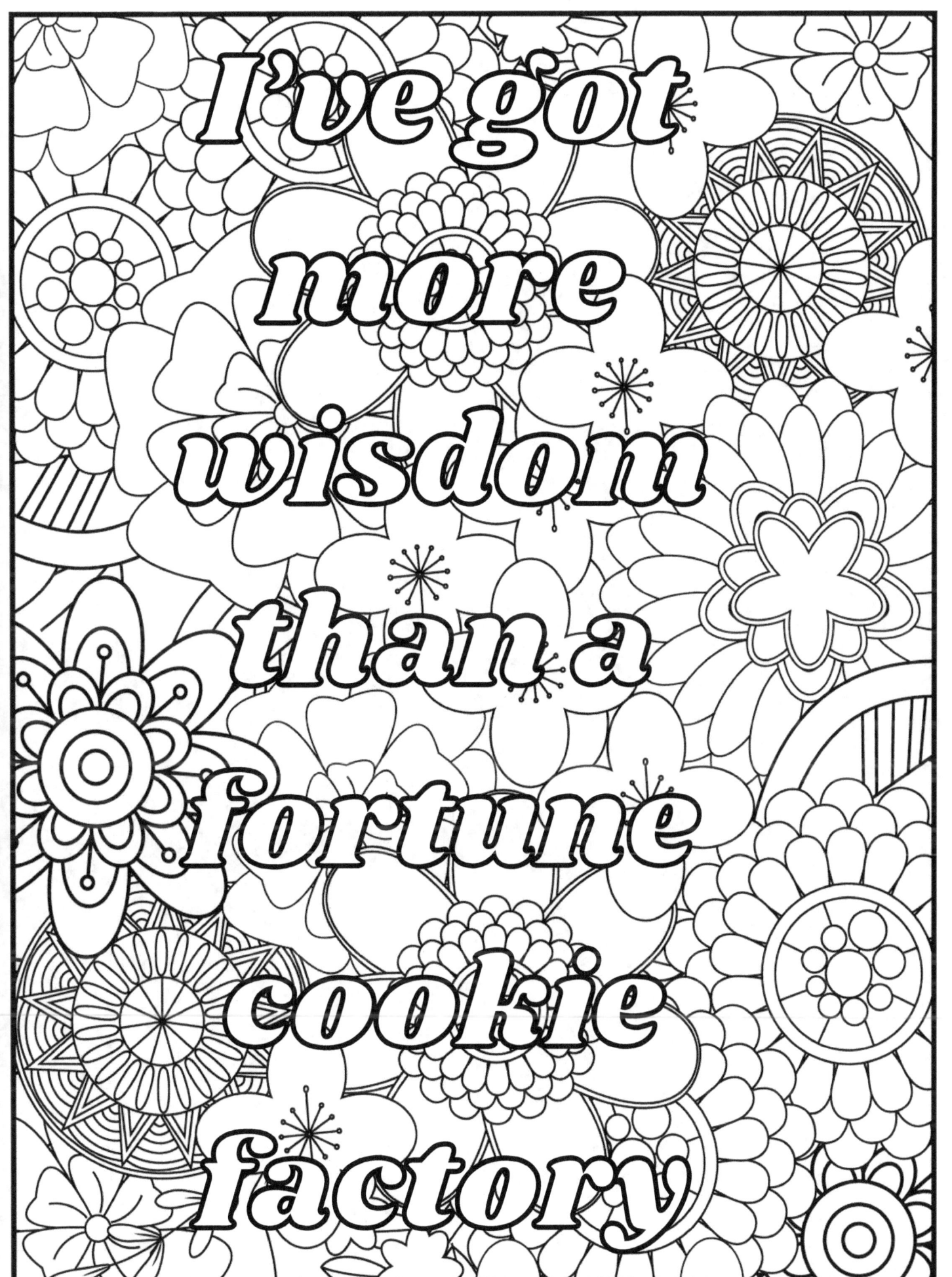

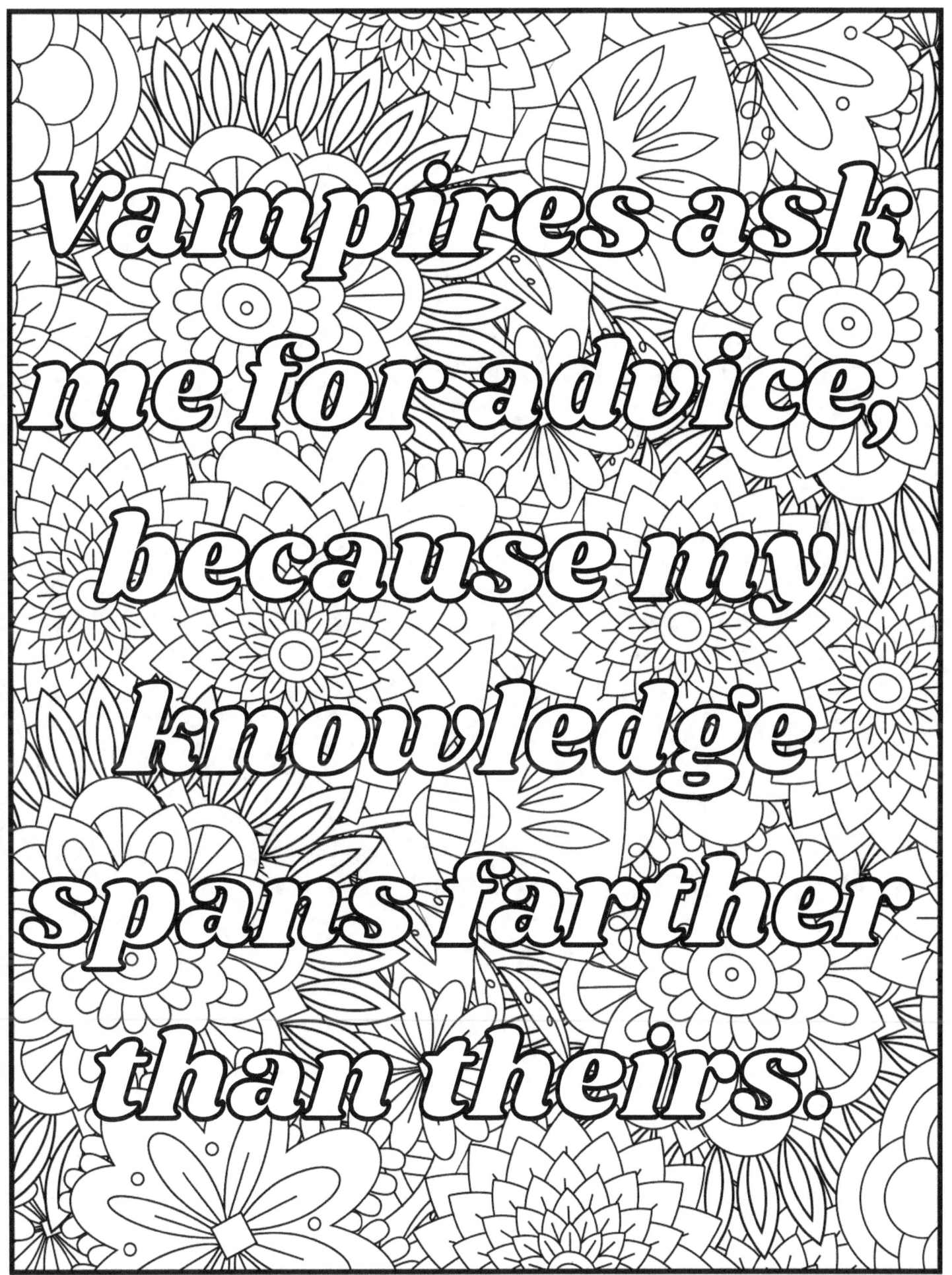

ENJOYED COLORING THIS?

GET MORE BOOKS FROM THE AUTHOR

Scan this with your Camera